THE VISUAL
DICTIONARY *of*
ANIMALS

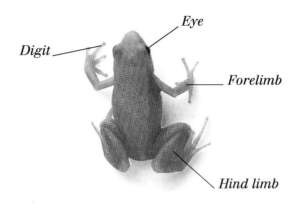

Eye

Digit

Forelimb

Hind limb

**EXTERNAL FEATURES
OF A FROG**

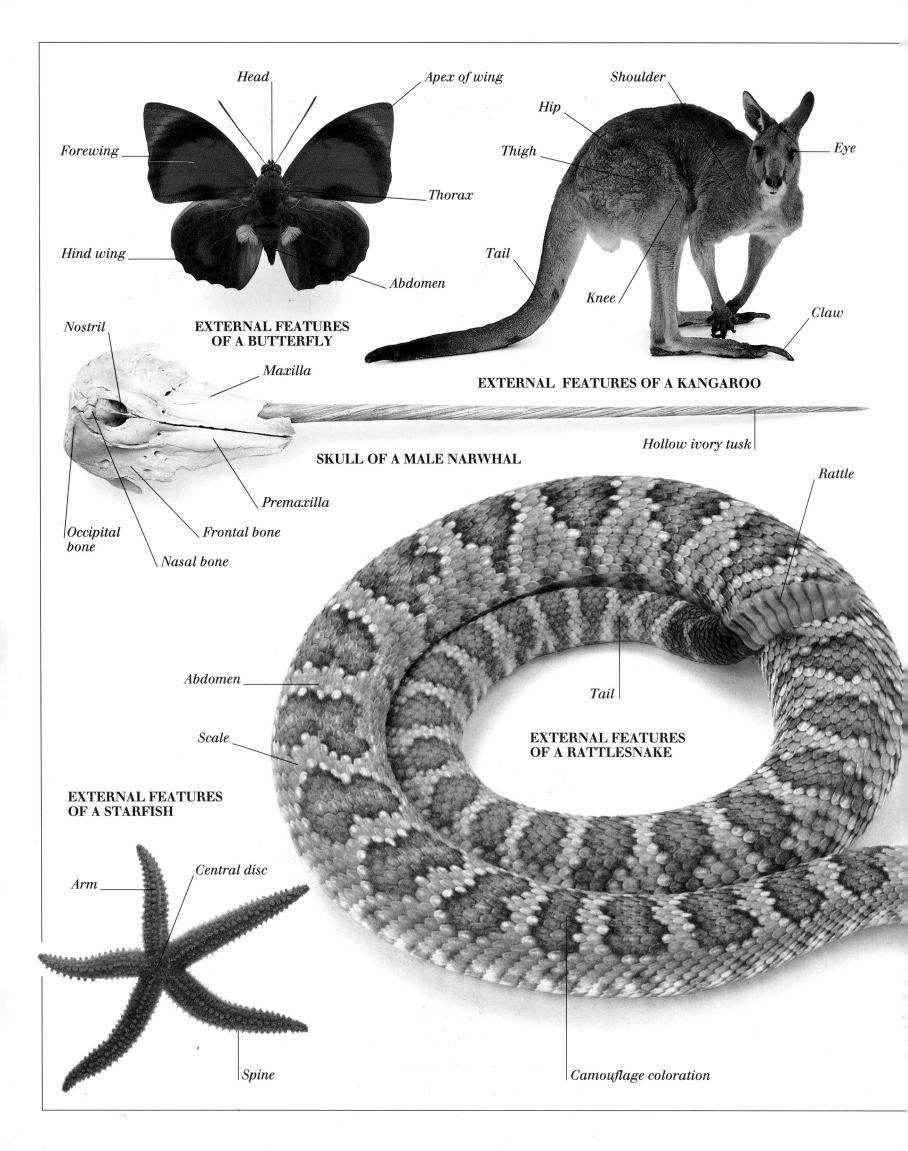

Head

Apex of wing

Shoulder

Hip

Forewing

Thigh

Eye

Thorax

Hind wing

Tail

Abdomen

Knee

Claw

**EXTERNAL FEATURES
OF A BUTTERFLY**

EXTERNAL FEATURES OF A KANGAROO

Nostril

Maxilla

Hollow ivory tusk

SKULL OF A MALE NARWHAL

Rattle

Premaxilla

Occipital
bone

Frontal bone

Nasal bone

Abdomen

Tail

Scale

**EXTERNAL FEATURES
OF A RATTLESNAKE**

**EXTERNAL FEATURES
OF A STARFISH**

Arm

Central disc

Spine

Camouflage coloration

EYEWITNESS VISUAL DICTIONARIES

THE VISUAL
DICTIONARY *of*
ANIMALS

Eye

Nuchal shield

Head

Marginal shield

Central shield
(Vertebral shield)

Lateral shield
(costal shield)

Pygal shield

**EXTERNAL FEATURES
OF A TERRAPIN**

DORLING KINDERSLEY
LONDON • NEW YORK • STUTTGART

A DORLING KINDERSLEY BOOK

PROJECT ART EDITOR CLARE SHEDDEN
DESIGNER ANDREW NASH

PROJECT EDITOR MARTYN PAGE
CONSULTANT EDITOR DR RICHARD WALKER

SERIES ART EDITOR PAUL WILKINSON
ART DIRECTOR CHEZ PICTHALL
MANAGING EDITOR RUTH MIDGLEY

PHOTOGRAPHY DAVE KING, GEOFF DANN
ILLUSTRATIONS JOHN WOODCOCK, SIMONE END

PRODUCTION HILARY STEPHENS

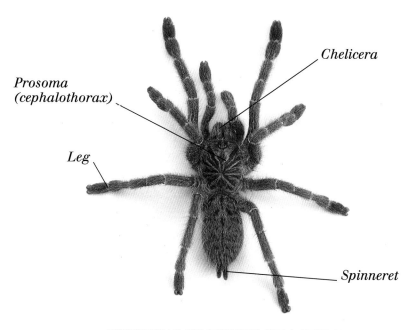

Chelicera

*Prosoma
(cephalothorax)*

Leg

Spinneret

EXTERNAL FEATURES OF A SPIDER

FIRST PUBLISHED IN GREAT BRITAIN IN 1991
BY DORLING KINDERSLEY LIMITED,
9 HENRIETTA STREET, LONDON WC2E 8PS

REPRINTED 1992

A CIP CATALOGUE RECORD FOR THIS BOOK IS AVAILABLE FROM THE BRITISH LIBRARY

ISBN 0-86318-701-3

REPRODUCED BY GRB GRAFICA, VERONA, ITALY
PRINTED AND BOUND BY ARNOLDO MONDADORI, VERONA, ITALY

Contents

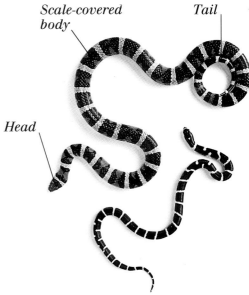

Scale-covered body

Tail

Head

EXTERNAL FEATURES OF A SNAKE

Digit

Hind limb

Forelimb

EXTERNAL FEATURES OF A FROG

ANIMAL BODIES   6

ANIMAL HEADS   8

BUTTERFLIES AND MOTHS   10

BEETLES, ANTS, AND BEES   12

ARACHNIDS   14

WORMS, FLUKES, AND LEECHES   16

SHARKS AND JAWLESS FISH   18

BONY FISH   20

STARFISH AND SEA URCHINS   22

SPONGES, JELLYFISH, AND SEA ANEMONES   24

MOLLUSCS   26

CRUSTACEANS   28

AMPHIBIANS   30

LIZARDS AND SNAKES   32

CROCODILIANS AND TURTLES   34

BIRDS   36

EGGS   40

CARNIVORES   42

RABBITS AND RODENTS   44

UNGULATES   46

ELEPHANTS   48

PRIMATES   50

DOLPHINS, WHALES, AND SEALS   52

MARSUPIALS AND MONOTREMES   54

ANIMAL TRACKS   56

ANIMAL CLASSIFICATION   58

INDEX   60

ACKNOWLEDGMENTS   64

Carapace (shell)

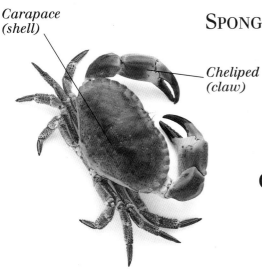

Cheliped (claw)

EXTERNAL FEATURES OF A CRAB

Back

Eye

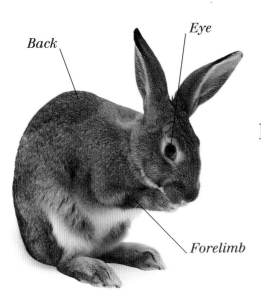

Forelimb

EXTERNAL FEATURES OF A RABBIT

Skull

Scapula

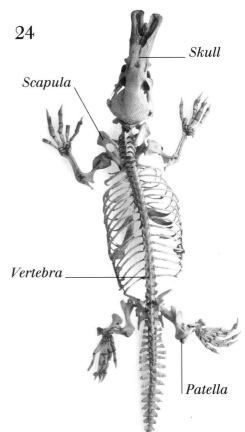

Vertebra

Patella

SKELETON OF A PLATYPUS

Hind flipper

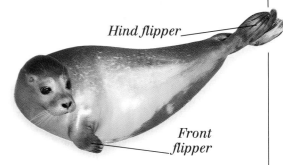

Front flipper

EXTERNAL FEATURES OF A SEAL

Animal bodies

THE BODY OF AN ANIMAL reflects the animal's way of life and the habitat in which it lives. Some marine creatures, such as squid and mackerel, have smooth, streamlined bodies to enable them to move rapidly through water, whereas the slower-moving starfish creeps over the seabed using its many tube feet. Most land animals have limbs for support and movement, although snakes move their long, scale-covered bodies without the need for legs. Frogs have powerful hind limbs for jumping; their webbed feet and thin, moist skin are adaptations to living in wet places. The beetle's six jointed legs support a heavy body covered by a hard, protective exoskeleton (external skeleton). The tiger's strong legs, sharp teeth, and forward-facing eyes mark it out as a hunter, as do the kestrel's powerful wings, sharp talons, and hooked beak.

Thin, moist skin

Forelimb

Eye

Web

TREE FROG
(Hyla arborea)
An amphibian

Long, powerful hind limb

Pinna (ear flap)

Forward-facing eye

Nose

Mouth

Vibrissa (whisker)

LONGHORN BEETLE
(Calipogen barbatus)
An insect

TIGER
(Panthera tigris)
A carnivorous (flesh-eating) mammal

Mandible

Jointed leg

Compound eye

Hard exoskeleton
(external skeleton)

Sensory
antenna

Forelimb

COMMON ATLANTIC MACKEREL
(Scomber scombrus)
A bony fish

Posterior dorsal fin

Anterior dorsal fin

Smooth, streamlined,
scale-covered body

Eye

Elytron
(wing case)

Caudal fin (tail)

Anal fin

Pectoral fin

Pelvic fin

Mouth

Operculum
(gill cover)

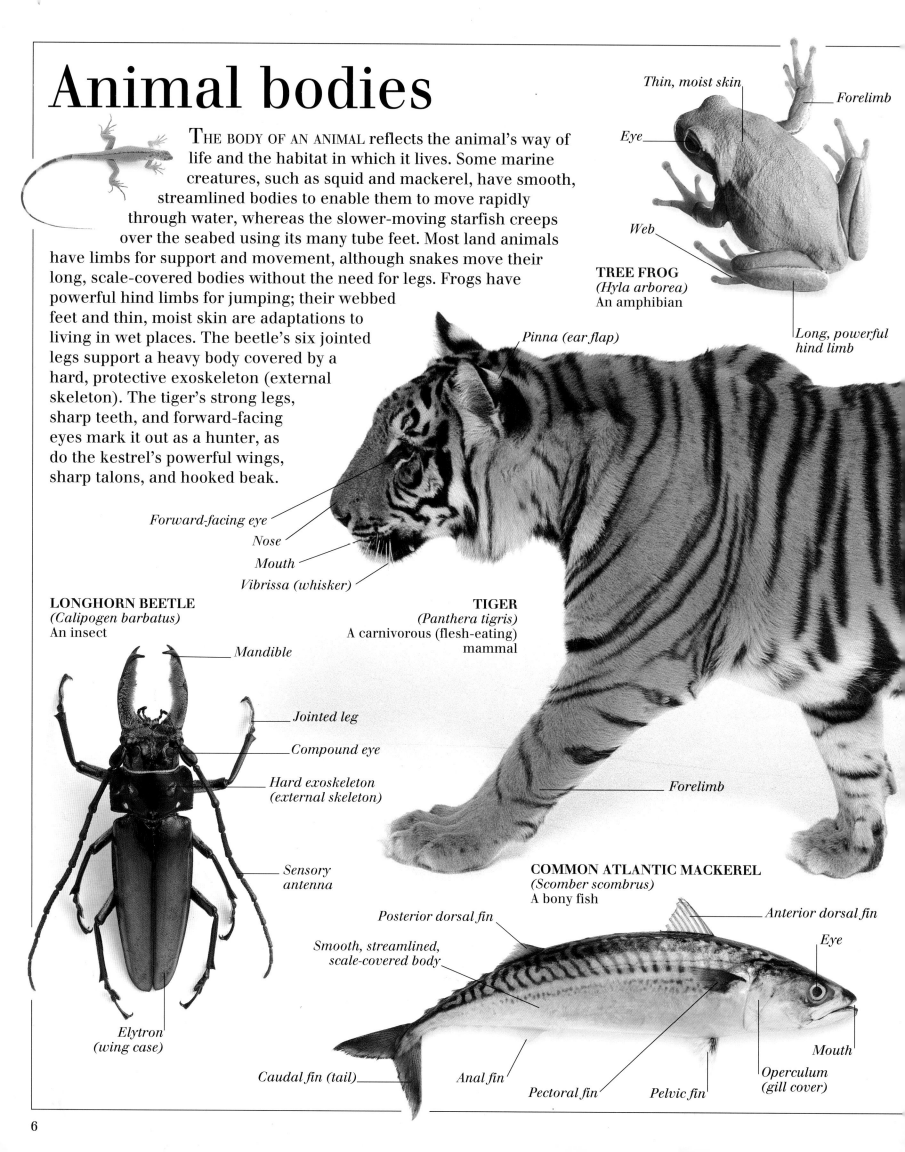

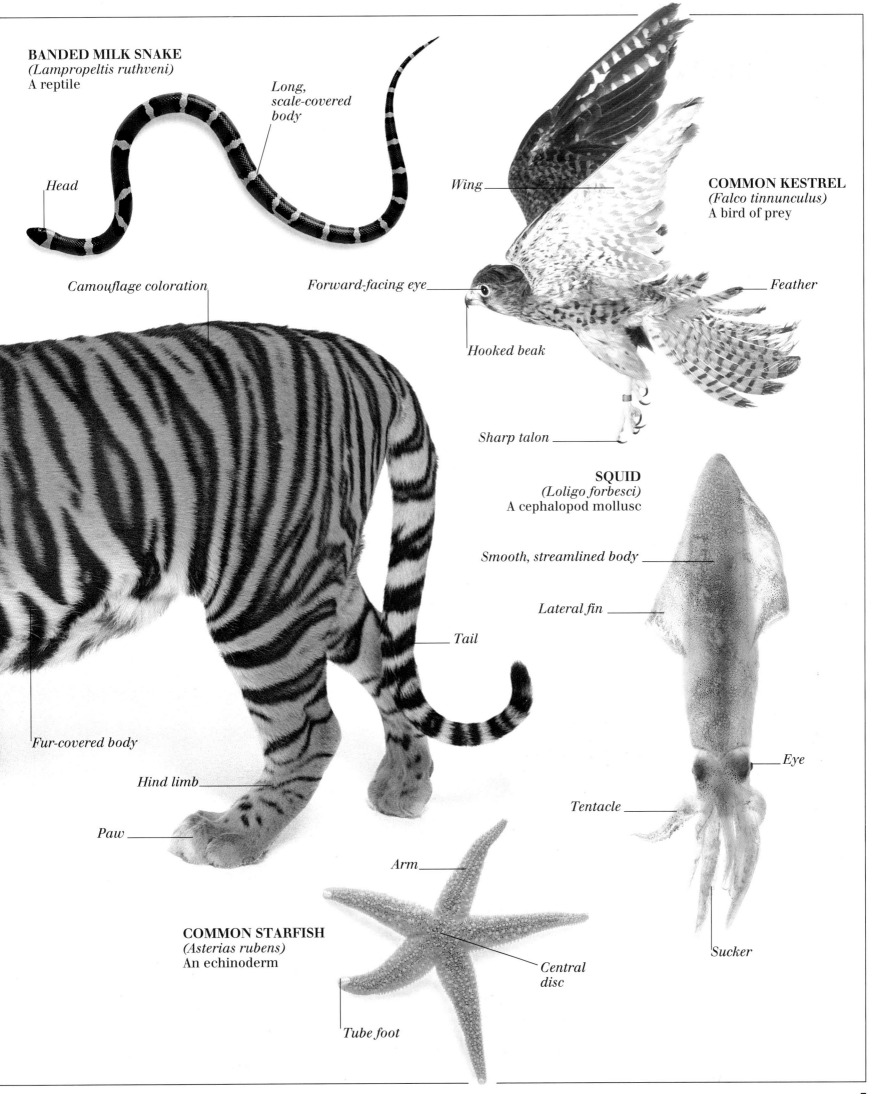

BANDED MILK SNAKE
(Lampropeltis ruthveni)
A reptile

Long,
scale-covered
body

Head

Camouflage coloration

Fur-covered body

Hind limb

Paw

Tail

COMMON KESTREL
(Falco tinnunculus)
A bird of prey

Wing

Feather

Forward-facing eye

Hooked beak

Sharp talon

SQUID
(Loligo forbesci)
A cephalopod mollusc

Smooth, streamlined body

Lateral fin

Eye

Tentacle

Sucker

Arm

COMMON STARFISH
(Asterias rubens)
An echinoderm

Central
disc

Tube foot

Animal heads

MOST ACTIVELY MOVING ANIMALS HAVE a definite head region at the front of their bodies. The head is usually the first part of an animal to receive information from the surroundings, and it therefore has several specialized sensory structures—eyes, ears, whiskers, and antennae, for example—to detect any changes in its surroundings. To enable the animal to react appropriately to external changes, sensory information is processed by the brain, which is located inside the head. In most higher animals, the head also has a mouth and a pair of nostrils. The mouth—and the teeth, if the animal has them—is used to capture and ingest food; it also contains taste buds to detect chemicals, and can be used for breathing. Similarly, the nostrils are used for breathing, and sensory structures in the nasal cavity detect odours.

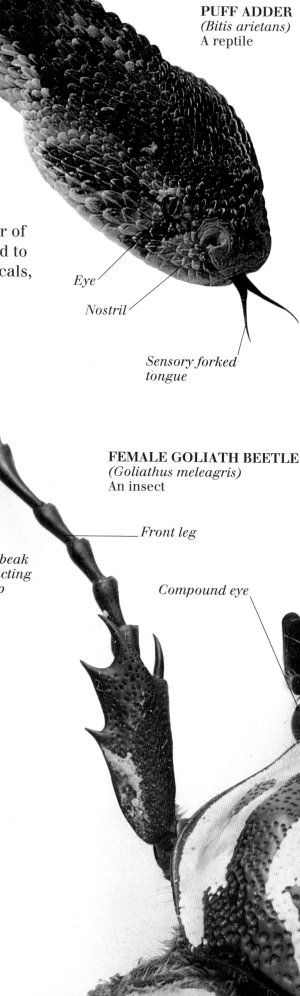

PUFF ADDER
(Bitis arietans)
A reptile

Eye

Nostril

Sensory forked
tongue

BLUE-STREAKED LORY
(Eos reticulata)
A seed- and fruit-eating bird

**BLUE-SPOTTED
SEA BREAM**
(Pagrus coerulostictus)
A bony fish

Eye

Nostril

FEMALE GOLIATH BEETLE
(Goliathus meleagris)
An insect

Front leg

Compound eye

Spine of
dorsal fin

Hook of beak
for extracting
fruit pulp

Broad base
of beak for
cracking seeds

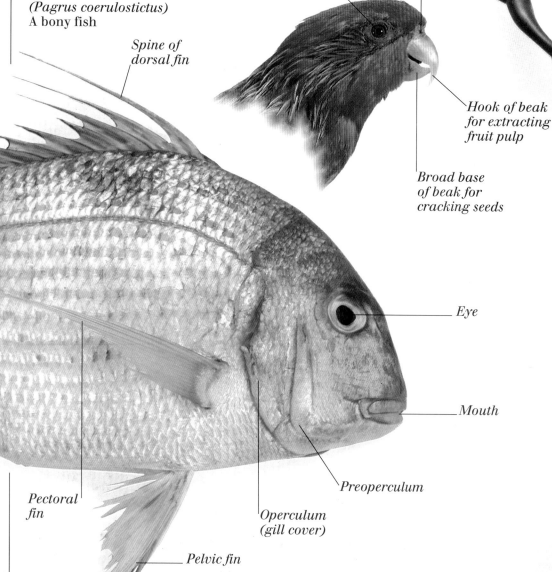

Eye

Mouth

Pectoral
fin

Preoperculum

Operculum
(gill cover)

Pelvic fin

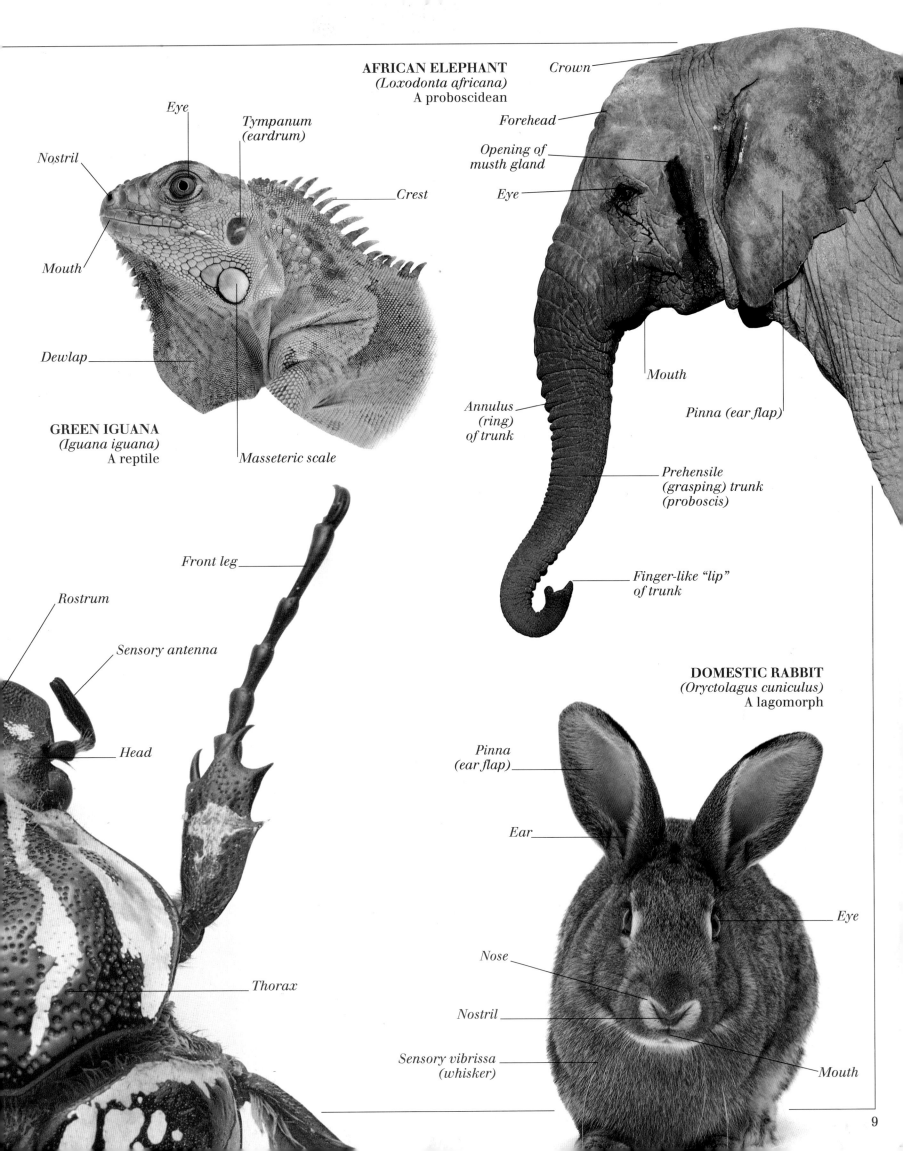

AFRICAN ELEPHANT
(Loxodonta africana)
A proboscidean

Crown

Forehead

Opening of musth gland

Eye

Mouth

Pinna (ear flap)

Annulus (ring) of trunk

Prehensile (grasping) trunk (proboscis)

Finger-like "lip" of trunk

Eye

Tympanum (eardrum)

Nostril

Crest

Mouth

Dewlap

GREEN IGUANA
(Iguana iguana)
A reptile

Masseteric scale

Front leg

Rostrum

Sensory antenna

Head

Thorax

DOMESTIC RABBIT
(Oryctolagus cuniculus)
A lagomorph

Pinna (ear flap)

Ear

Eye

Nose

Nostril

Sensory vibrissa (whisker)

Mouth

9

Butterflies and moths

BUTTERFLIES AND MOTHS FORM THE order Lepidoptera, one of the divisions of the large class Insecta, which is itself part of the even larger phylum Arthropoda. Lepidopterans are one of the biggest groups of insects, with about 150,000 species (about 15 per cent of all known insects). They are characterized by having wings covered with tiny scales, hence the name of their order (Lepidoptera means "scale wings"). Butterflies and moths also possess features that are common to all insects: an exoskeleton (external skeleton); three pairs of jointed legs, although the front pair are very small in some lepidopterans; three body sections (head, thorax, and abdomen); and one pair of sensory antennae. Like certain other insects (beetles, flies, and bees, for example), butterflies and moths undergo complete metamorphosis during their life-cycle.

DIFFERENCES BETWEEN BUTTERFLIES AND MOTHS

The separation of lepidopterans into butterflies and moths is largely artificial as there are no features that categorically distinguish one group from the other. In general, however, most butterflies fly by day, whereas most moths are night-flyers; butterflies tend to have clubbed antennae, whereas those of moths tend to be plain or feathery; butterflies usually rest with their wings upright over their backs, whereas moths rest with their wings flat; and butterflies tend to be more brightly coloured than moths.

MOTH

Plain antenna

Dull-coloured wings

BUTTERFLY

Clubbed antenna

Brightly coloured wings

EXTERNAL FEATURES OF A BUTTERFLY

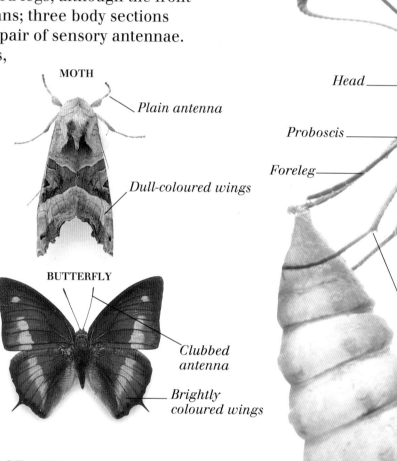

Antenna

Compound eye

Head

Proboscis

Foreleg

Thorax

Femur

Middle leg

Tibia

Hind leg

Tarsus

INTERNAL ANATOMY OF A FEMALE BUTTERFLY

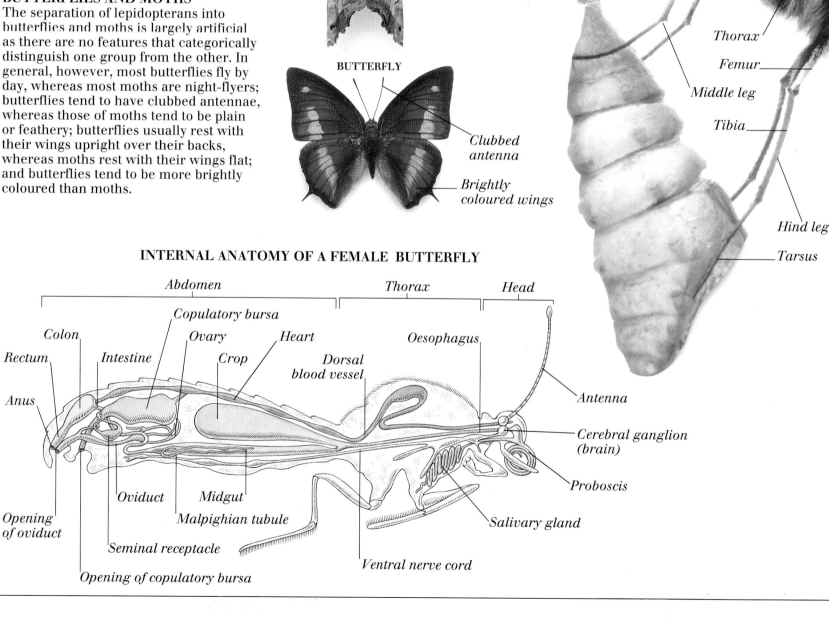

Abdomen

Thorax

Head

Copulatory bursa

Colon

Ovary

Heart

Oesophagus

Rectum

Intestine

Crop

Dorsal blood vessel

Anus

Antenna

Cerebral ganglion (brain)

Proboscis

Oviduct

Midgut

Opening of oviduct

Malpighian tubule

Salivary gland

Seminal receptacle

Ventral nerve cord

Opening of copulatory bursa

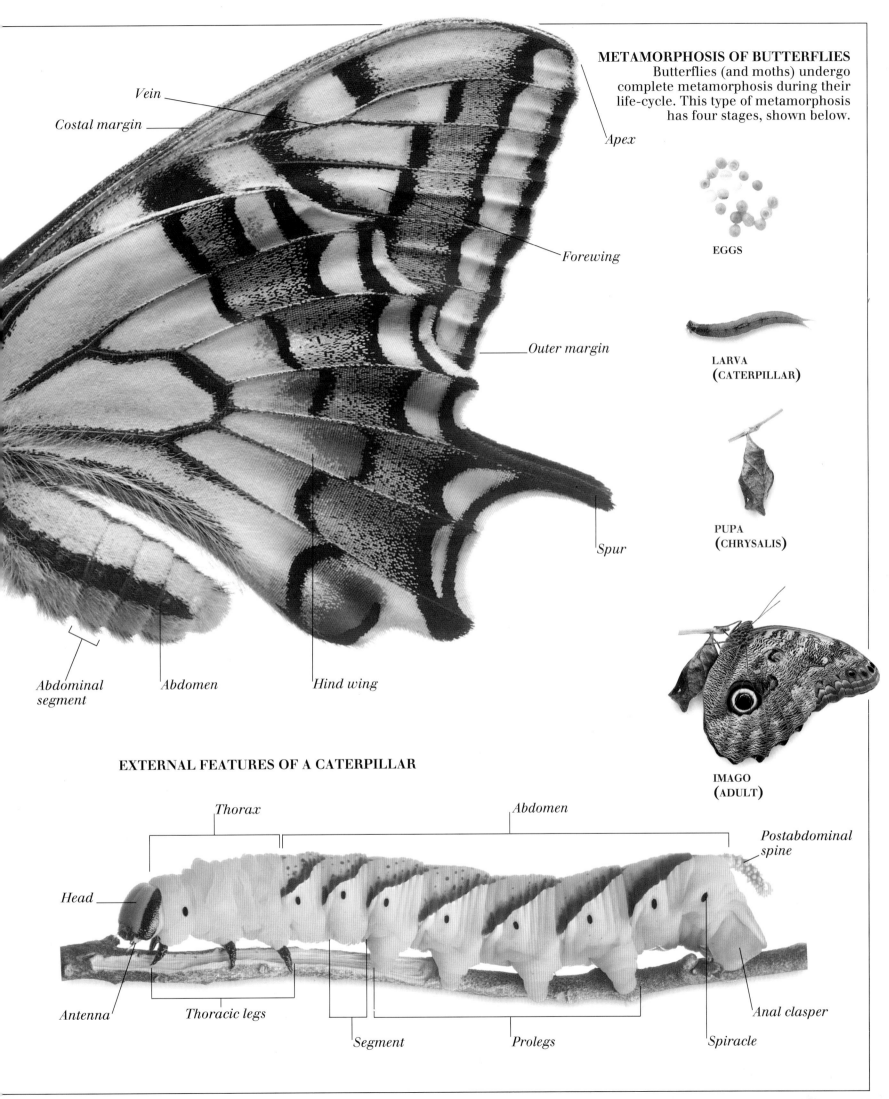

Vein

Costal margin

Apex

METAMORPHOSIS OF BUTTERFLIES
Butterflies (and moths) undergo complete metamorphosis during their life-cycle. This type of metamorphosis has four stages, shown below.

EGGS

Forewing

LARVA
(CATERPILLAR)

Outer margin

PUPA
(CHRYSALIS)

Spur

Abdominal
segment

Abdomen

Hind wing

IMAGO
(ADULT)

EXTERNAL FEATURES OF A CATERPILLAR

Thorax

Abdomen

Postabdominal
spine

Head

Antenna

Thoracic legs

Segment

Prolegs

Spiracle

Anal clasper

11

Beetles, ants, and bees

BEETLES, ANTS, AND BEES BELONG to different orders in the class Insecta, which is a division of the phylum Arthropoda. Beetles (order Coleoptera) are the biggest group of insects, with about 300,000 species. The characteristic feature of beetles is a pair of hard elytra (wing cases), which are modified front wings. The principal function of the elytra is to protect the hind wings, which are used for flying. Ants, together with bees and wasps, form the order Hymenoptera, which contains about 200,000 species. This group is characterized by a marked narrowing between the thorax and abdomen. Both of the above groups also have features common to all insects: an exoskeleton (external skeleton); three pairs of jointed legs; three body sections (head, thorax, and abdomen); and one pair of sensory antennae.

TYPES OF BEES

Some bees (bumblebees and honeybees, for example) exhibit polymorphism, that is, different types (or castes) of bees occur in the same species. Bumblebees have three castes: workers, which are sterile females; drones, which are fertile males; and queens, which are fertile females.

QUEEN BUMBLEBEE

DRONE BUMBLEBEE

WORKER BUMBLEBEE

EXTERNAL FEATURES OF A BUMBLEBEE

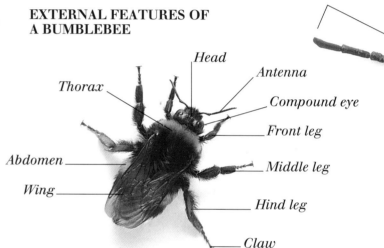

Head
Antenna
Thorax
Compound eye
Front leg
Abdomen
Middle leg
Wing
Hind leg
Claw

CHAFER BEETLE
(Neptunides polychromus)
Upper (dorsal) side

CHAFER BEETLE
(Neptunides polychromus)
Lower (ventral) side

EXAMPLES OF BEETLES

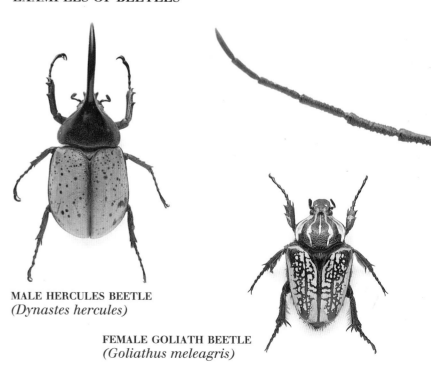

MALE ATLAS BEETLE
(Chalcosoma atlas)

MALE HERCULES BEETLE
(Dynastes hercules)

FEMALE GOLIATH BEETLE
(Goliathus meleagris)

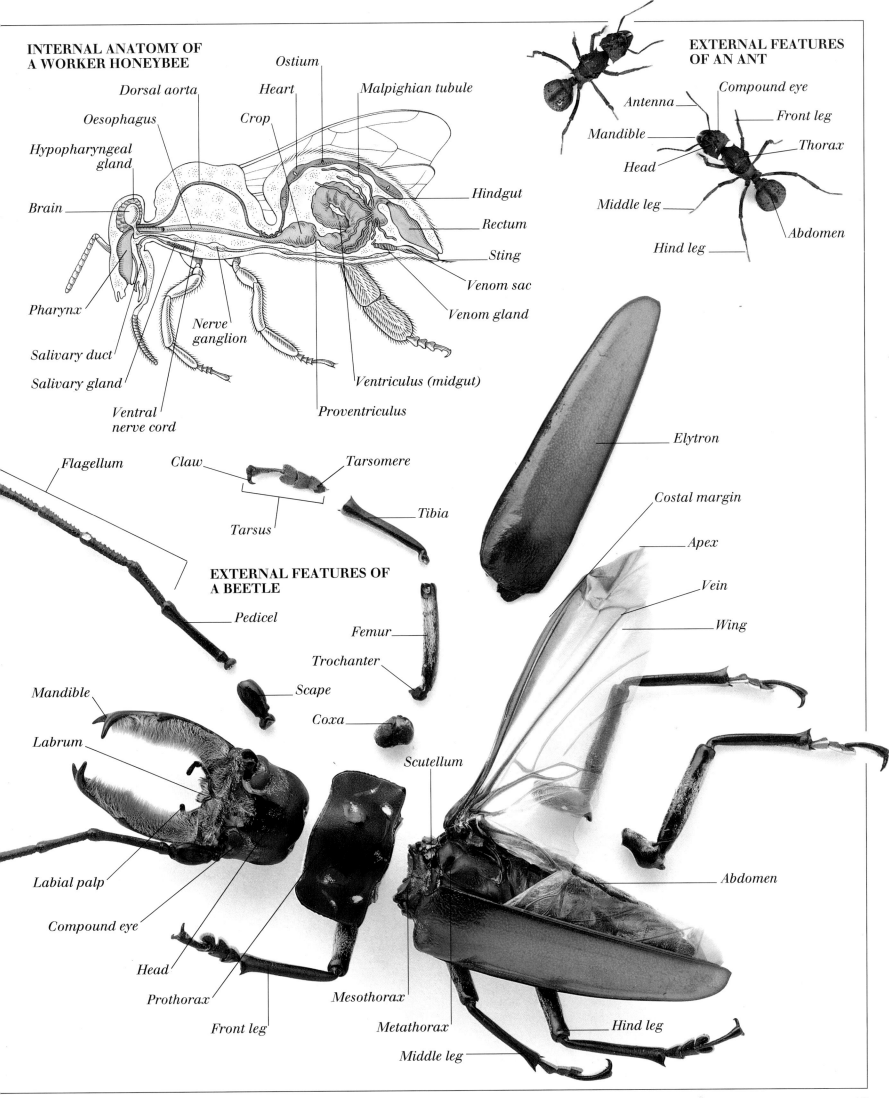

INTERNAL ANATOMY OF A WORKER HONEYBEE

Ostium

Dorsal aorta

Heart

Oesophagus

Crop

Malpighian tubule

Hypopharyngeal gland

Brain

Hindgut

Rectum

Sting

Venom sac

Venom gland

Pharynx

Nerve ganglion

Salivary duct

Salivary gland

Ventriculus (midgut)

Ventral nerve cord

Proventriculus

EXTERNAL FEATURES OF AN ANT

Compound eye

Antenna

Front leg

Mandible

Thorax

Head

Middle leg

Abdomen

Hind leg

Elytron

Flagellum

Claw

Tarsomere

Costal margin

Tibia

Apex

Tarsus

Vein

EXTERNAL FEATURES OF A BEETLE

Wing

Pedicel

Femur

Trochanter

Scape

Mandible

Coxa

Labrum

Scutellum

Labial palp

Abdomen

Compound eye

Head

Prothorax

Mesothorax

Front leg

Metathorax

Hind leg

Middle leg

Arachnids

THE CLASS ARACHNIDA INCLUDES SPIDERS (order Araneae) and
scorpions (order Scorpiones). The class is part of the phylum
Arthropoda, which also includes insects and crustaceans.

Spiders and scorpions are characterized by having four pairs of
walking legs; a pair of pincer-like mouthparts called chelicerae; another
pair of frontal appendages called pedipalps, which are sensory in spiders
but used for grasping in scorpions; and a body divided into two
sections (a combined head and thorax called a cephalothorax
or prosoma, and an abdomen or opisthosoma).
Unlike other arthropods, spiders and
scorpions lack antennae. Spiders
and scorpions are carnivorous.
Spiders poison prey by biting
with the fanged chelicerae,
scorpions by stinging
with the end of the
metasoma (tail).

**MEXICAN TRUE RED-
LEGGED TARANTULA**
(Euathlus emilia)

INTERNAL ANATOMY OF A FEMALE SPIDER

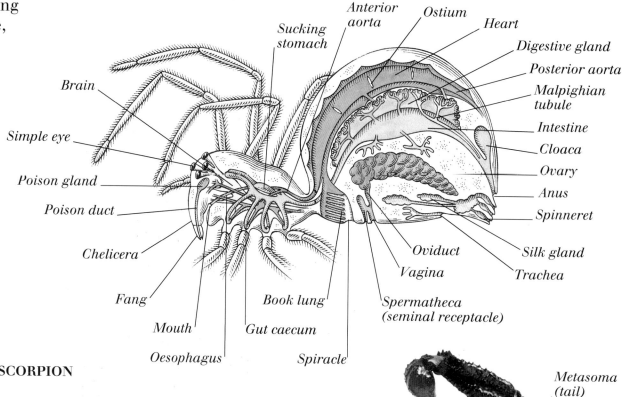

Brain
Simple eye
Poison gland
Poison duct
Chelicera
Fang
Mouth
Oesophagus

Sucking
stomach
Anterior
aorta
Ostium
Heart

Digestive gland
Posterior aorta
Malpighian
tubule
Intestine
Cloaca
Ovary
Anus
Spinneret
Silk gland
Trachea

Book lung
Gut caecum
Spiracle
Oviduct
Vagina
Spermatheca
(seminal receptacle)

EXTERNAL FEATURES OF A SCORPION

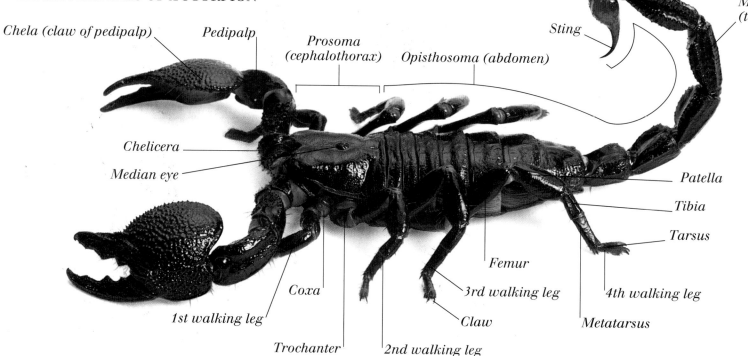

Chela (claw of pedipalp)
Pedipalp
Prosoma
(cephalothorax)
Opisthosoma (abdomen)
Sting
Metasoma
(tail)

Chelicera
Median eye

Patella
Tibia
Tarsus

Coxa
1st walking leg
Trochanter
2nd walking leg
Claw
Femur
3rd walking leg
Metatarsus
4th walking leg

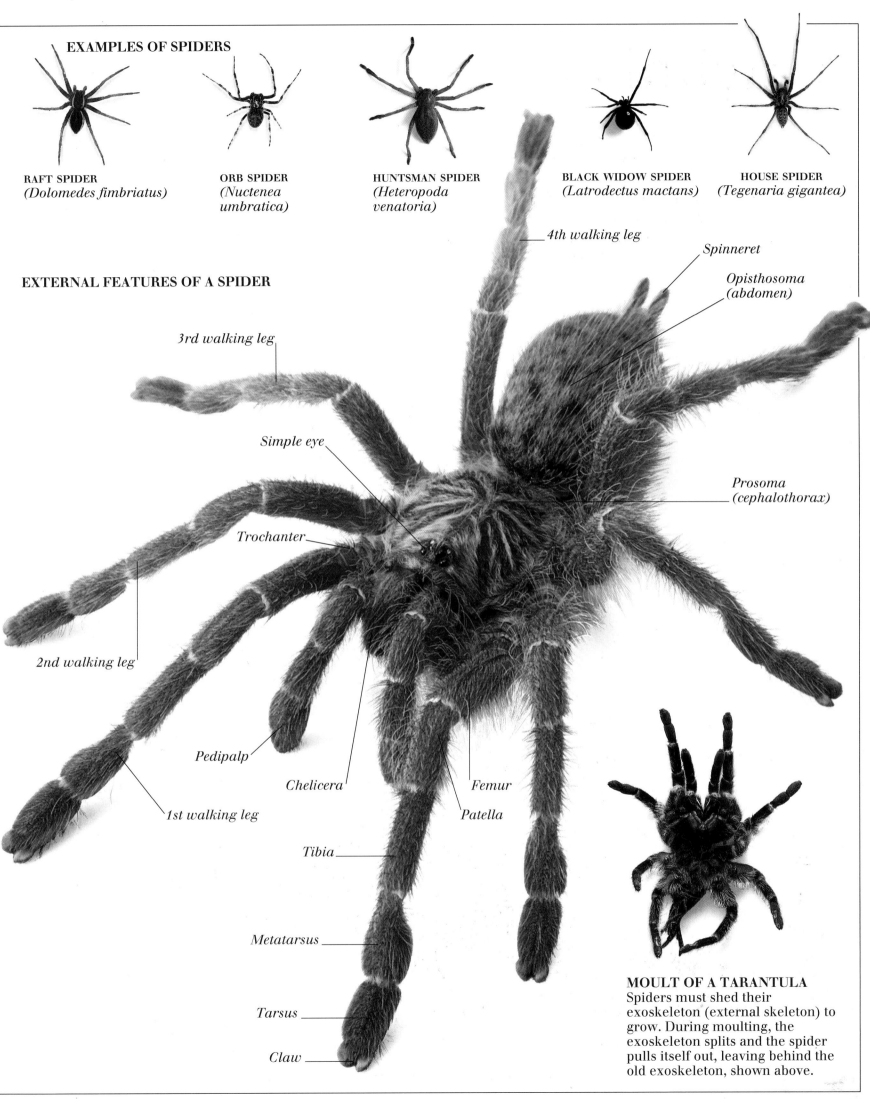

EXAMPLES OF SPIDERS

RAFT SPIDER
(Dolomedes fimbriatus)

ORB SPIDER
*(Nuctenea
umbratica)*

HUNTSMAN SPIDER
*(Heteropoda
venatoria)*

BLACK WIDOW SPIDER
(Latrodectus mactans)

HOUSE SPIDER
(Tegenaria gigantea)

EXTERNAL FEATURES OF A SPIDER

4th walking leg

Spinneret

*Opisthosoma
(abdomen)*

3rd walking leg

Simple eye

*Prosoma
(cephalothorax)*

Trochanter

2nd walking leg

Pedipalp

Chelicera

Femur

Patella

1st walking leg

Tibia

Metatarsus

Tarsus

Claw

MOULT OF A TARANTULA
Spiders must shed their
exoskeleton (external skeleton) to
grow. During moulting, the
exoskeleton splits and the spider
pulls itself out, leaving behind the
old exoskeleton, shown above.

Worms, flukes, and leeches

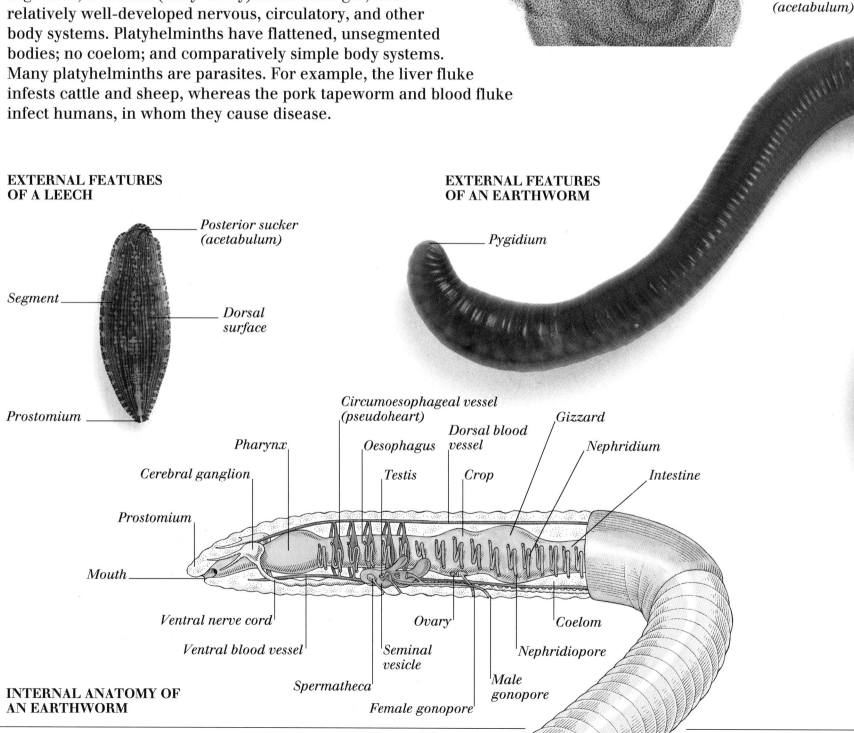

THE TERM "WORM" HAS NO STRICT SCIENTIFIC meaning, but it is commonly applied to various long, thin, soft-bodied animals. Probably the best-known groups of worms are the segmented worms (phylum Annelida), which include earthworms, marine worms such as sandworms and ragworms, and also leeches; and the flatworms (phylum Platyhelminthes), which include tapeworms and flukes. Annelid worms have cylindrical bodies divided into many segments; a coelom (body cavity) around the gut; and relatively well-developed nervous, circulatory, and other body systems. Platyhelminths have flattened, unsegmented bodies; no coelom; and comparatively simple body systems. Many platyhelminths are parasites. For example, the liver fluke infests cattle and sheep, whereas the pork tapeworm and blood fluke infect humans, in whom they cause disease.

HEAD (SCOLEX) OF A PORK TAPEWORM

Rostellum

Hook

Sucker (acetabulum)

EXTERNAL FEATURES OF A LEECH

Posterior sucker (acetabulum)

Segment

Dorsal surface

Prostomium

EXTERNAL FEATURES OF AN EARTHWORM

Pygidium

INTERNAL ANATOMY OF AN EARTHWORM

Pharynx

Cerebral ganglion

Prostomium

Mouth

Ventral nerve cord

Ventral blood vessel

Spermatheca

Female gonopore

Circumoesophageal vessel (pseudoheart)

Oesophagus

Testis

Dorsal blood vessel

Crop

Ovary

Seminal vesicle

Male gonopore

Gizzard

Nephridium

Intestine

Coelom

Nephridiopore

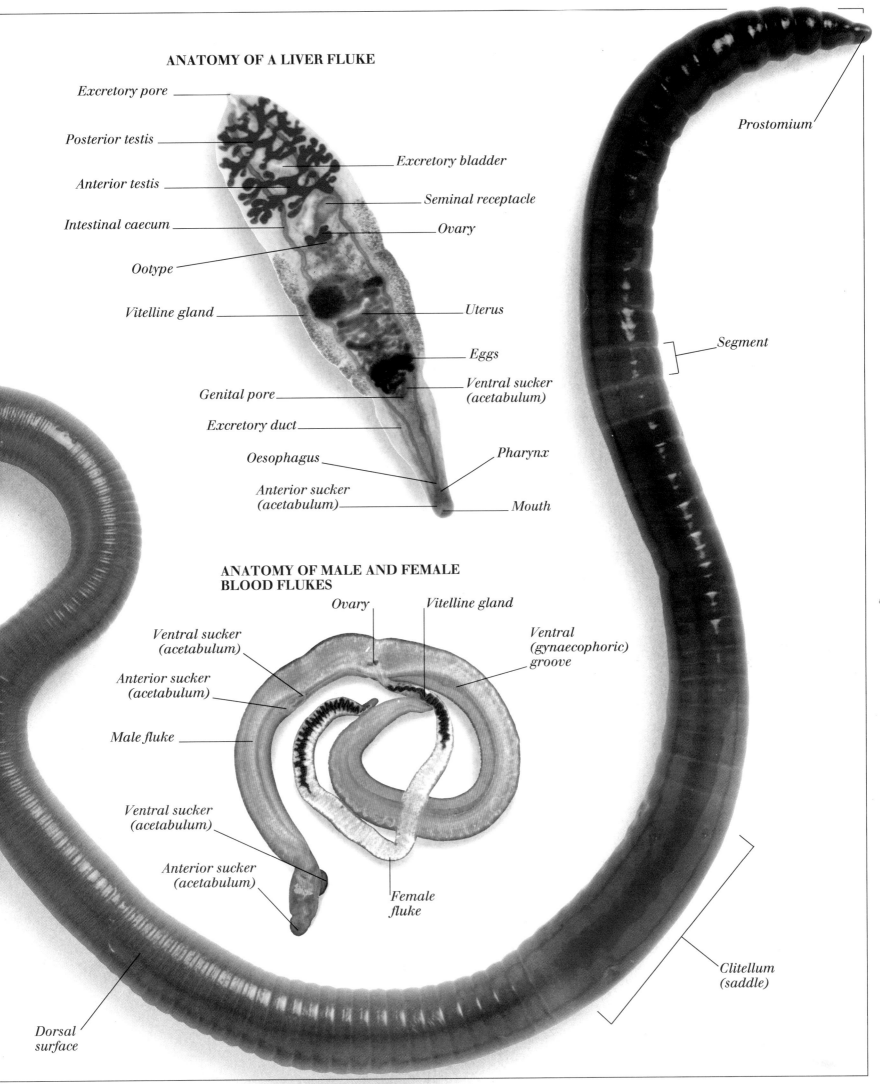

ANATOMY OF A LIVER FLUKE

Excretory pore

Posterior testis

Anterior testis

Intestinal caecum

Ootype

Vitelline gland

Genital pore

Excretory duct

Oesophagus

Anterior sucker
(acetabulum)

Excretory bladder

Seminal receptacle

Ovary

Uterus

Eggs

Ventral sucker
(acetabulum)

Pharynx

Mouth

ANATOMY OF MALE AND FEMALE
BLOOD FLUKES

Ovary

Vitelline gland

Ventral sucker
(acetabulum)

Anterior sucker
(acetabulum)

Male fluke

Ventral sucker
(acetabulum)

Anterior sucker
(acetabulum)

Ventral
(gynaecophoric)
groove

Female
fluke

Prostomium

Segment

Clitellum
(saddle)

Dorsal
surface

Sharks and jawless fish

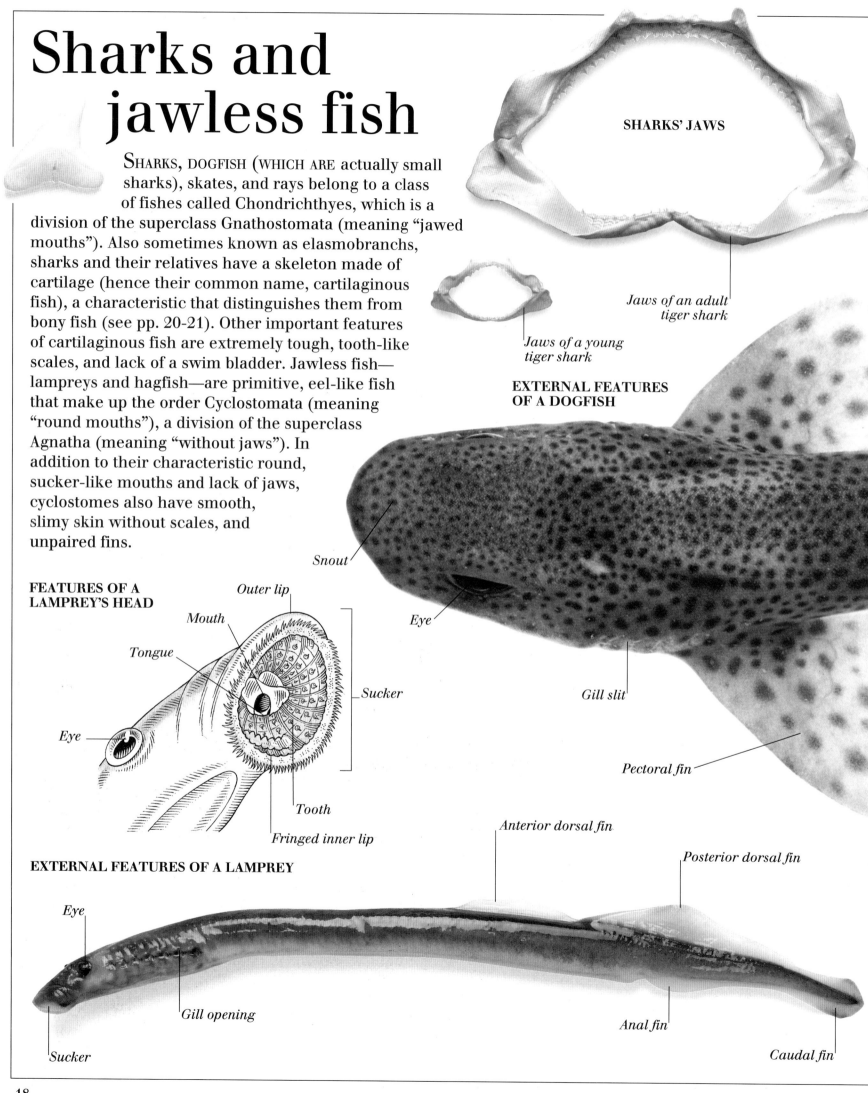

SHARKS, DOGFISH (WHICH ARE actually small sharks), skates, and rays belong to a class of fishes called Chondrichthyes, which is a division of the superclass Gnathostomata (meaning "jawed mouths"). Also sometimes known as elasmobranchs, sharks and their relatives have a skeleton made of cartilage (hence their common name, cartilaginous fish), a characteristic that distinguishes them from bony fish (see pp. 20-21). Other important features of cartilaginous fish are extremely tough, tooth-like scales, and lack of a swim bladder. Jawless fish—lampreys and hagfish—are primitive, eel-like fish that make up the order Cyclostomata (meaning "round mouths"), a division of the superclass Agnatha (meaning "without jaws"). In addition to their characteristic round, sucker-like mouths and lack of jaws, cyclostomes also have smooth, slimy skin without scales, and unpaired fins.

SHARKS' JAWS

Jaws of an adult tiger shark

Jaws of a young tiger shark

EXTERNAL FEATURES OF A DOGFISH

Snout

Eye

Gill slit

Pectoral fin

FEATURES OF A LAMPREY'S HEAD

Outer lip

Mouth

Tongue

Sucker

Eye

Tooth

Fringed inner lip

EXTERNAL FEATURES OF A LAMPREY

Eye

Gill opening

Sucker

Anterior dorsal fin

Posterior dorsal fin

Anal fin

Caudal fin

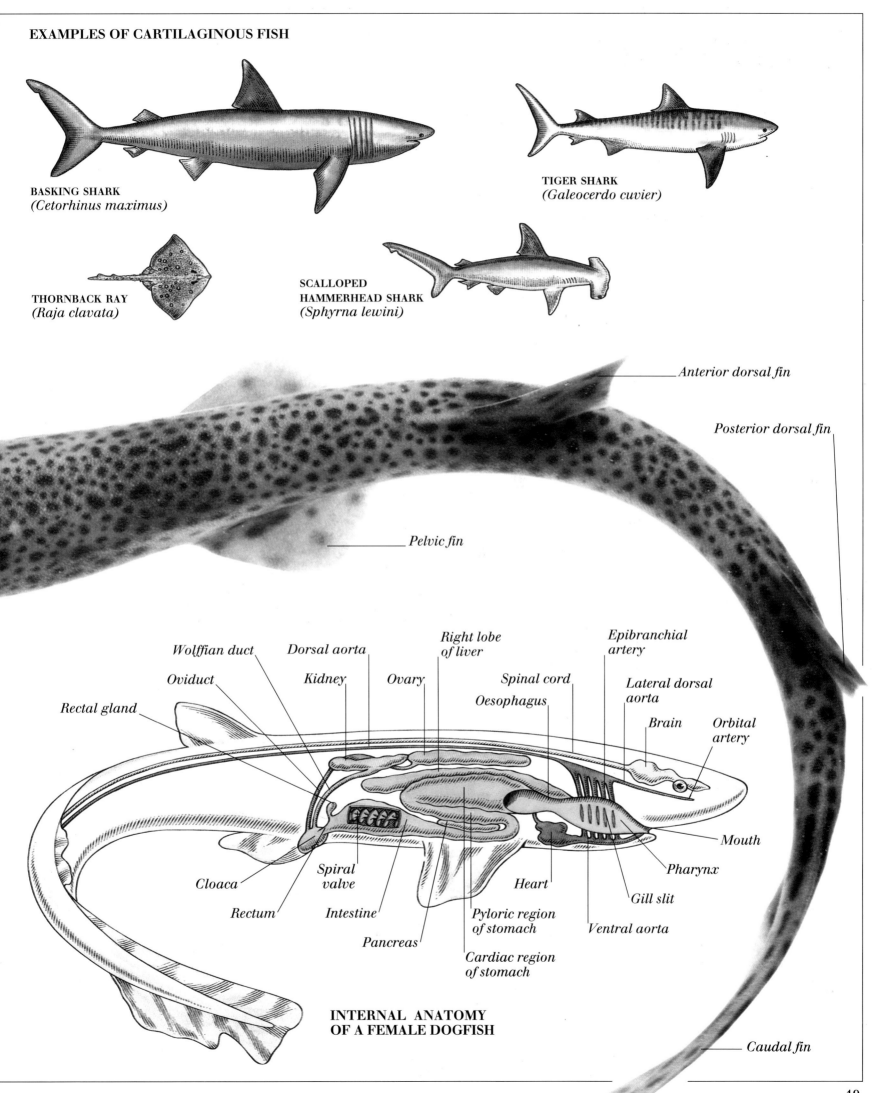

EXAMPLES OF CARTILAGINOUS FISH

BASKING SHARK
(Cetorhinus maximus)

TIGER SHARK
(Galeocerdo cuvier)

THORNBACK RAY
(Raja clavata)

**SCALLOPED
HAMMERHEAD SHARK**
(Sphyrna lewini)

Anterior dorsal fin

Posterior dorsal fin

Pelvic fin

Wolffian duct

Dorsal aorta

Right lobe
of liver

Epibranchial
artery

Oviduct

Kidney

Ovary

Spinal cord

Lateral dorsal
aorta

Rectal gland

Oesophagus

Brain

Orbital
artery

Mouth

Cloaca

Spiral
valve

Pharynx

Rectum

Intestine

Heart

Gill slit

Pancreas

Pyloric region
of stomach

Ventral aorta

Cardiac region
of stomach

**INTERNAL ANATOMY
OF A FEMALE DOGFISH**

Caudal fin

Bony fish

Bony fish, such as carp, trout, salmon, perch, and cod, are by far the best known and largest group of fish, with more than 20,000 species (over 95 per cent of all known fish). As their name suggests, bony fish have skeletons made of bone, in contrast to the cartilaginous skeletons of sharks, jawless fish, and their relatives (see pp. 18-19). Other typical features of bony fish include a swim bladder, which functions as a variable-buoyancy organ, enabling a fish to remain effortlessly at whatever depth it is swimming; relatively thin, bone-like scales; a flap (called an operculum) covering the gills; and paired pelvic and pectoral fins. Scientifically, bony fish belong to the class Osteichthyes, which is a division of the superclass Gnathostomata (meaning "jawed mouths").

HOW FISH BREATHE

Fish "breathe" by extracting oxygen from water through their gills. Water is sucked in through the mouth; simultaneously, the opercula close to prevent the water from escaping. The mouth is then closed, and muscles in the walls of the mouth, pharynx, and opercular cavity contract to pump the water inside over the gills and out through the opercula. Some fish rely on swimming with their mouths open to keep water flowing over the gills.

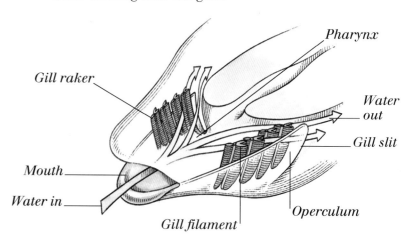

Pharynx

Gill raker

Water out

Gill slit

Mouth

Water in

Operculum

Gill filament

EXAMPLES OF BONY FISH

MANDARINFISH
(Synchiropus splendidus)

ANGLERFISH
(Caulophryne jordani)

LIONFISH
(Pterois volitans)

OCEANIC SEAHORSE
(Hippocampus kuda)

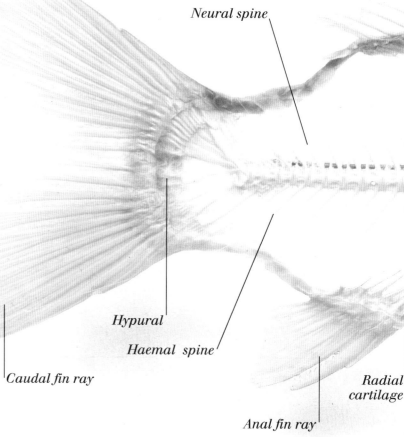

Vertebra

Neural spine

Hypural

Haemal spine

Caudal fin ray

Anal fin ray

Radial cartilage

STURGEON
(Acipenser sturio)

SNOWFLAKE MORAY EEL
(Echidna nebulosa)

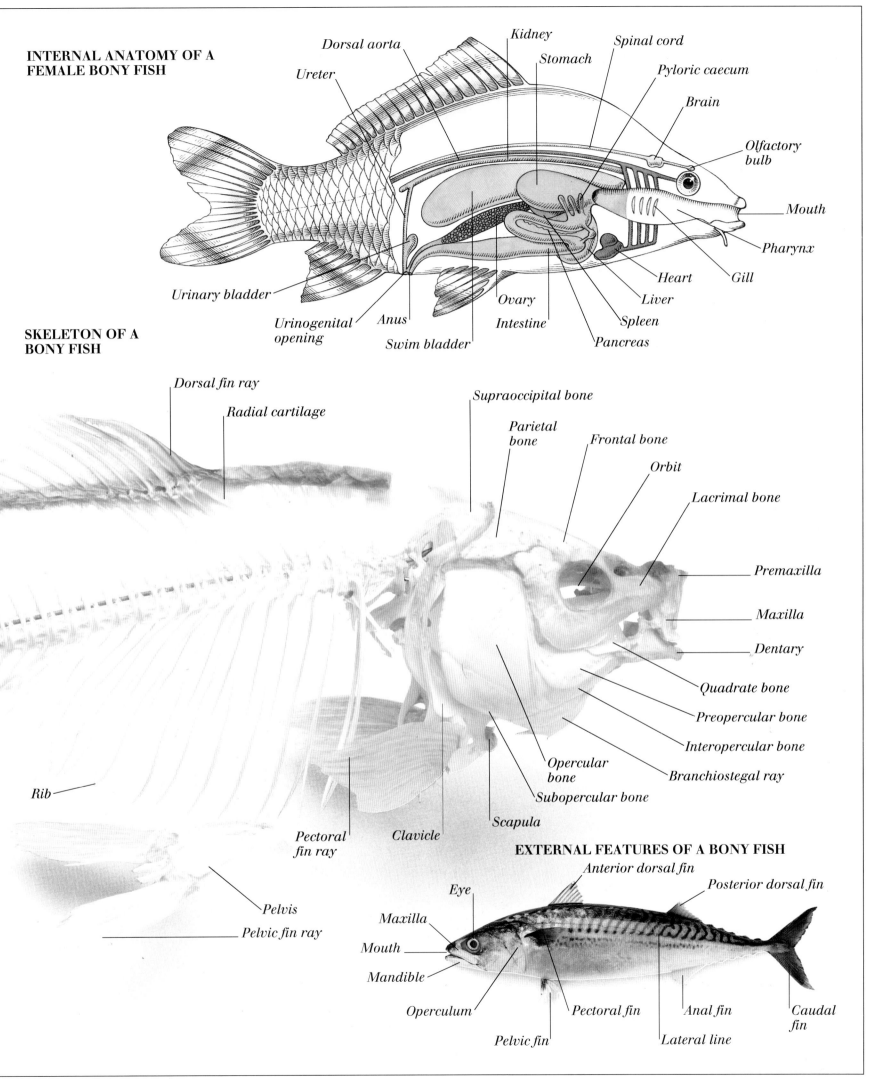

INTERNAL ANATOMY OF A FEMALE BONY FISH

Dorsal aorta
Ureter
Kidney
Stomach
Spinal cord
Pyloric caecum
Brain
Olfactory bulb
Mouth
Pharynx
Gill
Heart
Liver
Spleen
Pancreas
Intestine
Swim bladder
Ovary
Anus
Urinogenital opening
Urinary bladder

SKELETON OF A BONY FISH

Dorsal fin ray
Radial cartilage
Supraoccipital bone
Parietal bone
Frontal bone
Orbit
Lacrimal bone
Premaxilla
Maxilla
Dentary
Quadrate bone
Preopercular bone
Interopercular bone
Branchiostegal ray
Opercular bone
Subopercular bone
Scapula
Clavicle
Pectoral fin ray
Rib
Pelvis
Pelvic fin ray

EXTERNAL FEATURES OF A BONY FISH

Anterior dorsal fin
Posterior dorsal fin
Eye
Maxilla
Mouth
Mandible
Operculum
Pelvic fin
Pectoral fin
Lateral line
Anal fin
Caudal fin

21

Starfish and sea urchins

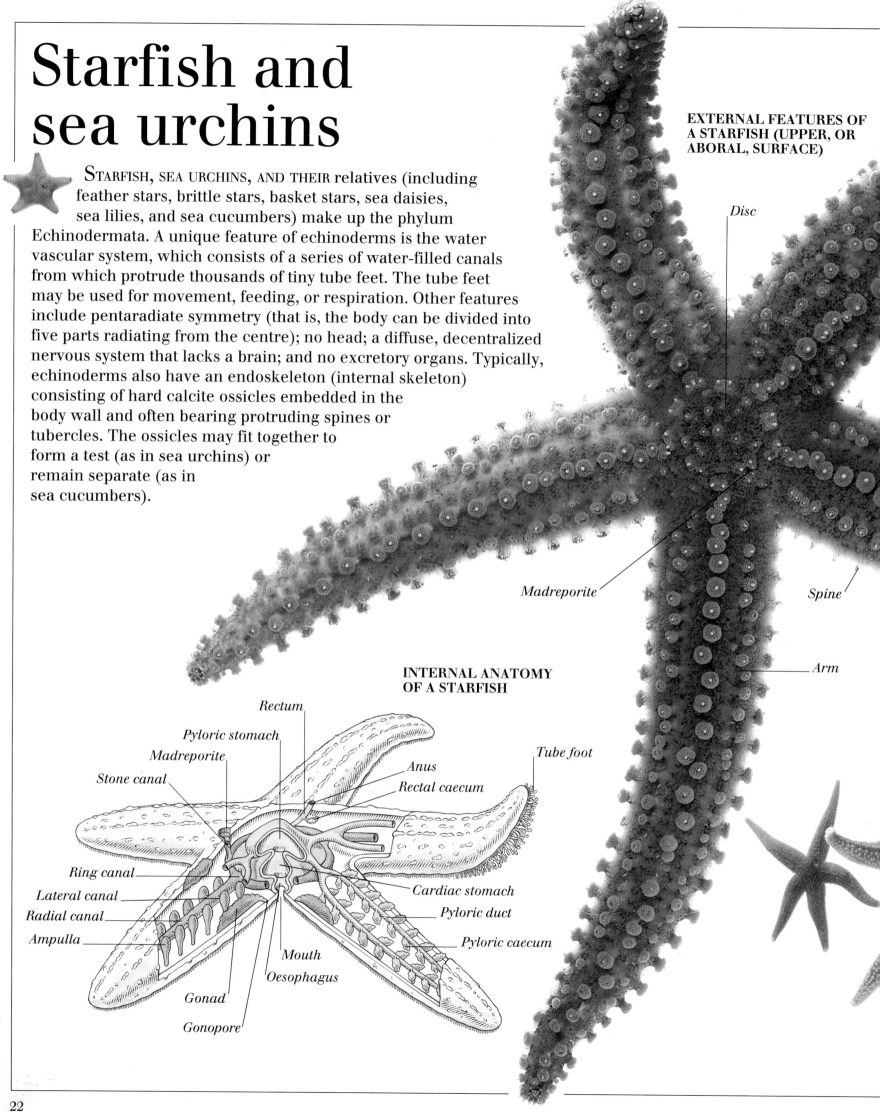

STARFISH, SEA URCHINS, AND THEIR relatives (including feather stars, brittle stars, basket stars, sea daisies, sea lilies, and sea cucumbers) make up the phylum Echinodermata. A unique feature of echinoderms is the water vascular system, which consists of a series of water-filled canals from which protrude thousands of tiny tube feet. The tube feet may be used for movement, feeding, or respiration. Other features include pentaradiate symmetry (that is, the body can be divided into five parts radiating from the centre); no head; a diffuse, decentralized nervous system that lacks a brain; and no excretory organs. Typically, echinoderms also have an endoskeleton (internal skeleton) consisting of hard calcite ossicles embedded in the body wall and often bearing protruding spines or tubercles. The ossicles may fit together to form a test (as in sea urchins) or remain separate (as in sea cucumbers).

EXTERNAL FEATURES OF A STARFISH (UPPER, OR ABORAL, SURFACE)

Disc

Madreporite

Spine

Arm

INTERNAL ANATOMY OF A STARFISH

Rectum

Pyloric stomach

Madreporite

Stone canal

Ring canal

Lateral canal

Radial canal

Ampulla

Mouth

Oesophagus

Gonad

Gonopore

Anus

Rectal caecum

Tube foot

Cardiac stomach

Pyloric duct

Pyloric caecum

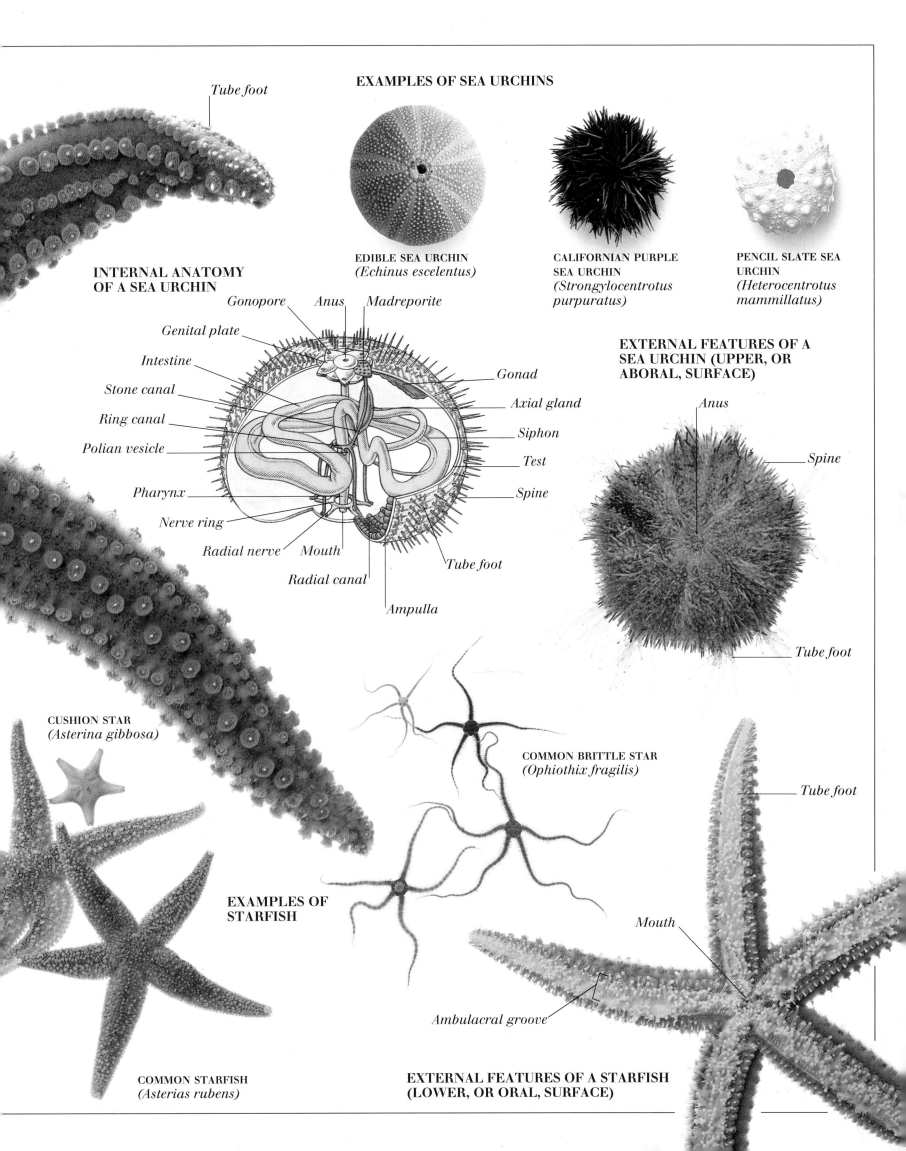

Tube foot

EXAMPLES OF SEA URCHINS

EDIBLE SEA URCHIN
(Echinus escelentus)

**CALIFORNIAN PURPLE
SEA URCHIN**
*(Strongylocentrotus
purpuratus)*

**PENCIL SLATE SEA
URCHIN**
*(Heterocentrotus
mammillatus)*

INTERNAL ANATOMY
OF A SEA URCHIN

Gonopore
Anus
Madreporite
Genital plate
Intestine
Stone canal
Ring canal
Polian vesicle
Pharynx
Nerve ring
Radial nerve
Mouth
Radial canal
Ampulla
Gonad
Axial gland
Siphon
Test
Spine
Tube foot

EXTERNAL FEATURES OF A
SEA URCHIN (UPPER, OR
ABORAL, SURFACE)

Anus
Spine
Tube foot

CUSHION STAR
(Asterina gibbosa)

COMMON BRITTLE STAR
(Ophiothix fragilis)

Tube foot

EXAMPLES OF
STARFISH

Mouth

Ambulacral groove

COMMON STARFISH
(Asterias rubens)

EXTERNAL FEATURES OF A STARFISH
(LOWER, OR ORAL, SURFACE)

Sponges, jellyfish, and sea anemones

SPONGES ARE MAINLY MARINE animals that make up the phylum Porifera. They are among the simplest of all animals, having no tissues or organs. Their bodies consist of two layers of cells separated by a jelly-like layer (mesohyal) that is strengthened by mineral spicules or protein fibres. The body is perforated by a system of pores and water channels called the aquiferous system. Special cells (choanocytes) with whip-like structures (flagella) draw water through the aquiferous system, thereby bringing tiny food particles to the sponge's cells. Jellyfish (class Scyphozoa), sea anemones (class Anthozoa), and corals (also class Anthozoa) belong to the phylum Cnidaria, also known as Coelenterata. More complex than sponges, coelenterates have simple tissues, such as nervous tissue; a radially symmetrical body; and a mouth surrounded by tentacles with unique stinging cells (cnidocytes).

INTERNAL ANATOMY OF A SPONGE

Amoebocyte

Osculum (excurrent pore)

Choanocyte (collar cell)

Ostium (incurrent pore)

Porocyte (pore cell)

Mesohyal

Spongocoel (atrium; paragaster)

Spicule

Pinacocyte (epidermal cell)

Ostium (incurrent pore)

SKELETON OF A SPONGE

EXTERNAL FEATURES OF A SEA ANEMONE

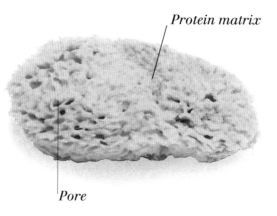

Protein matrix

Pore

Tentacle

EXAMPLES OF SEA ANEMONES

JEWEL ANEMONE
(Corynactis viridis)

PARASITIC ANEMONE
(Calliactis parasitica)

PLUMOSE ANEMONE
(Metridium senile)

MEDITERRANEAN SEA ANEMONE
(Condylactis sp.)

GREEN SNAKELOCK ANEMONE
(Anemonia viridis)

BEADLET ANEMONE
(Actinia equina)

GHOST ANEMONE
(Actinothoe sphyrodeta)

Sagartia elegans

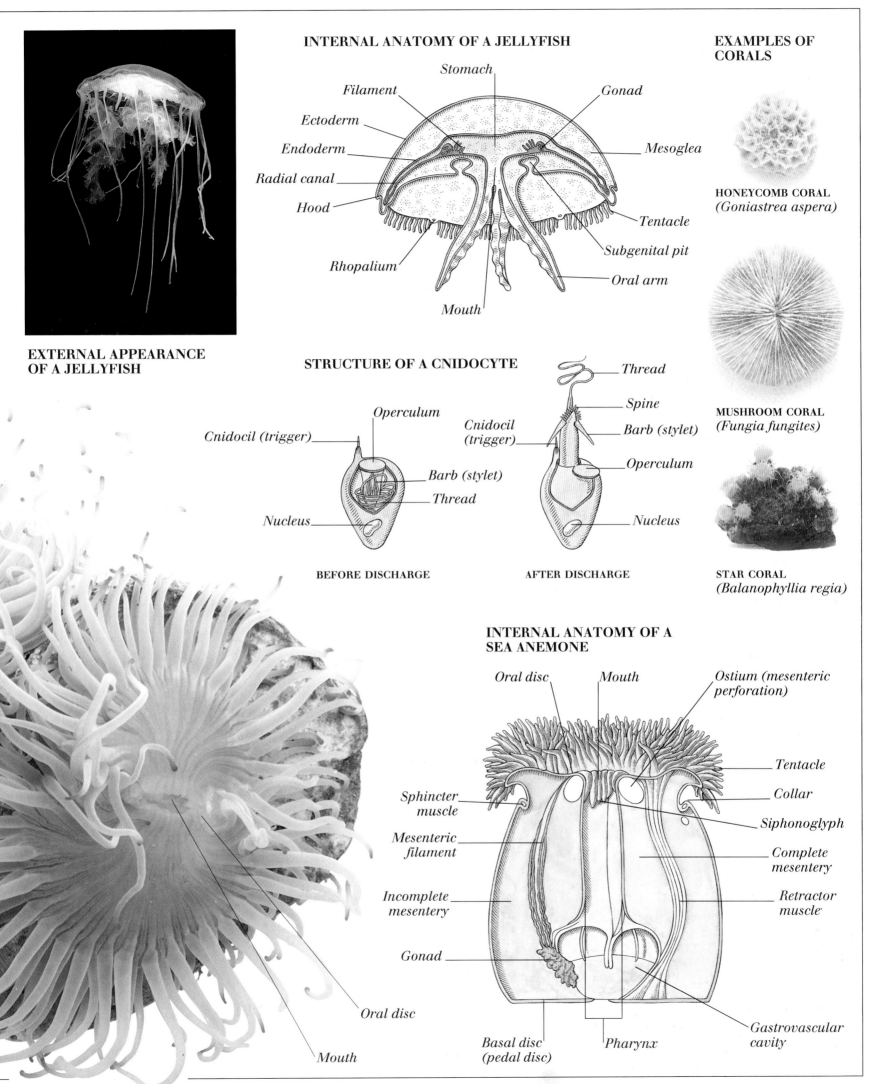

INTERNAL ANATOMY OF A JELLYFISH

Stomach

Filament

Gonad

Ectoderm

Endoderm

Mesoglea

Radial canal

Hood

Tentacle

Subgenital pit

Rhopalium

Oral arm

Mouth

**EXTERNAL APPEARANCE
OF A JELLYFISH**

**EXAMPLES OF
CORALS**

HONEYCOMB CORAL
(*Goniastrea aspera*)

MUSHROOM CORAL
(*Fungia fungites*)

STAR CORAL
(*Balanophyllia regia*)

STRUCTURE OF A CNIDOCYTE

Thread

Spine

Operculum

Cnidocil
(trigger)

Barb (stylet)

Cnidocil (trigger)

Operculum

Barb (stylet)

Thread

Nucleus

Nucleus

BEFORE DISCHARGE

AFTER DISCHARGE

**INTERNAL ANATOMY OF A
SEA ANEMONE**

Oral disc

Mouth

Ostium (mesenteric
perforation)

Tentacle

Sphincter
muscle

Collar

Siphonoglyph

Mesenteric
filament

Complete
mesentery

Incomplete
mesentery

Retractor
muscle

Gonad

Oral disc

Basal disc
(pedal disc)

Pharynx

Gastrovascular
cavity

Mouth

Molluscs

THE PHYLUM MOLLUSCA (MOLLUSCS) is a large group of animals that includes octopuses, snails, and scallops. Octopuses and their relatives —including squid and cuttlefish—form the class Cephalopoda. Cephalopods typically have a head with a radula (a file-like feeding organ) and beak; a well-developed nervous system; sucker-bearing tentacles; a muscular mantle (part of the body wall) that can expel water through the siphon, enabling movement by jet propulsion; and a small shell or no shell. Snails and their relatives—including slugs, limpets, and abalones—make up the class Gastropoda. Gastropods typically have a coiled external shell, although some, such as slugs, have a small internal shell or no shell; a flat foot; and a head with tentacles and a radula. Scallops and their relatives—including clams, mussels, and oysters—make up the class Bivalvia (also called Pelecypoda). Features of bivalves include a shell with two halves (valves); large gills that are used for breathing and filter feeding; and no radula.

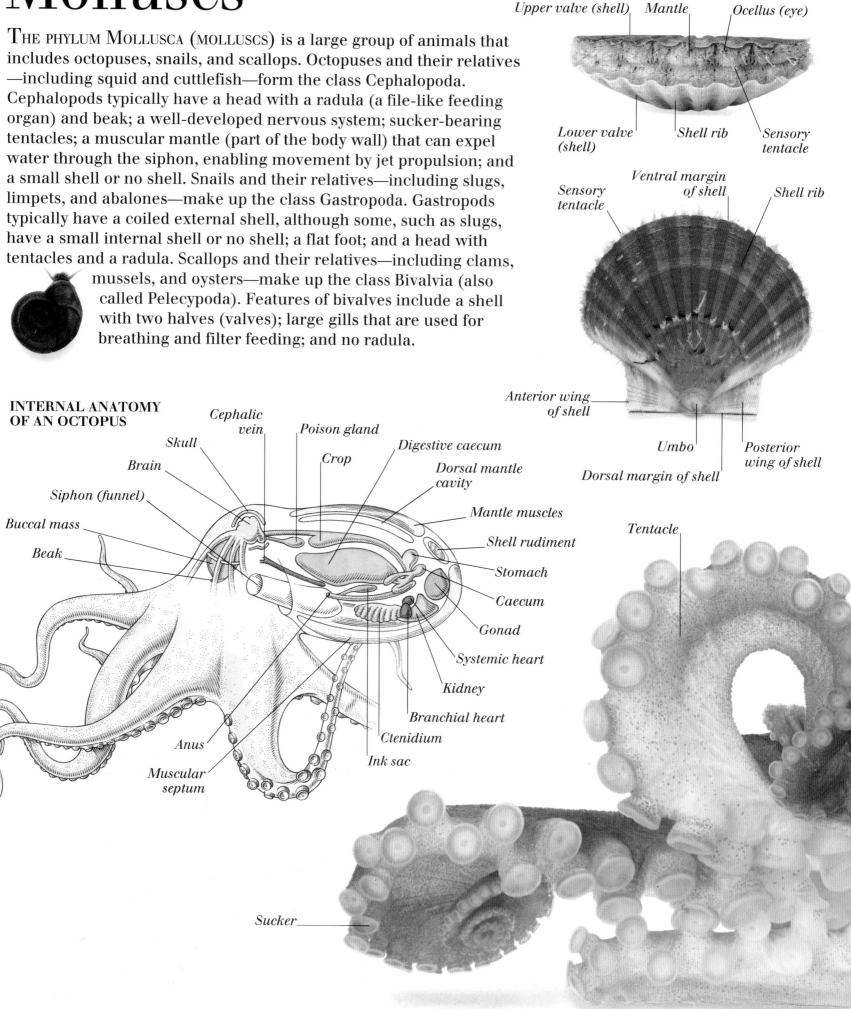

EXTERNAL FEATURES OF A SCALLOP

Upper valve (shell)   Mantle   Ocellus (eye)

Lower valve (shell)   Shell rib   Sensory tentacle

Sensory tentacle   Ventral margin of shell   Shell rib

Anterior wing of shell

Umbo   Posterior wing of shell

Dorsal margin of shell

Tentacle

INTERNAL ANATOMY OF AN OCTOPUS

Cephalic vein   Poison gland   Digestive caecum

Skull   Crop   Dorsal mantle cavity

Brain   Mantle muscles

Siphon (funnel)   Shell rudiment

Buccal mass   Stomach

Beak   Caecum

Gonad

Systemic heart

Kidney

Branchial heart

Ctenidium

Anus   Ink sac

Muscular septum

Sucker

26

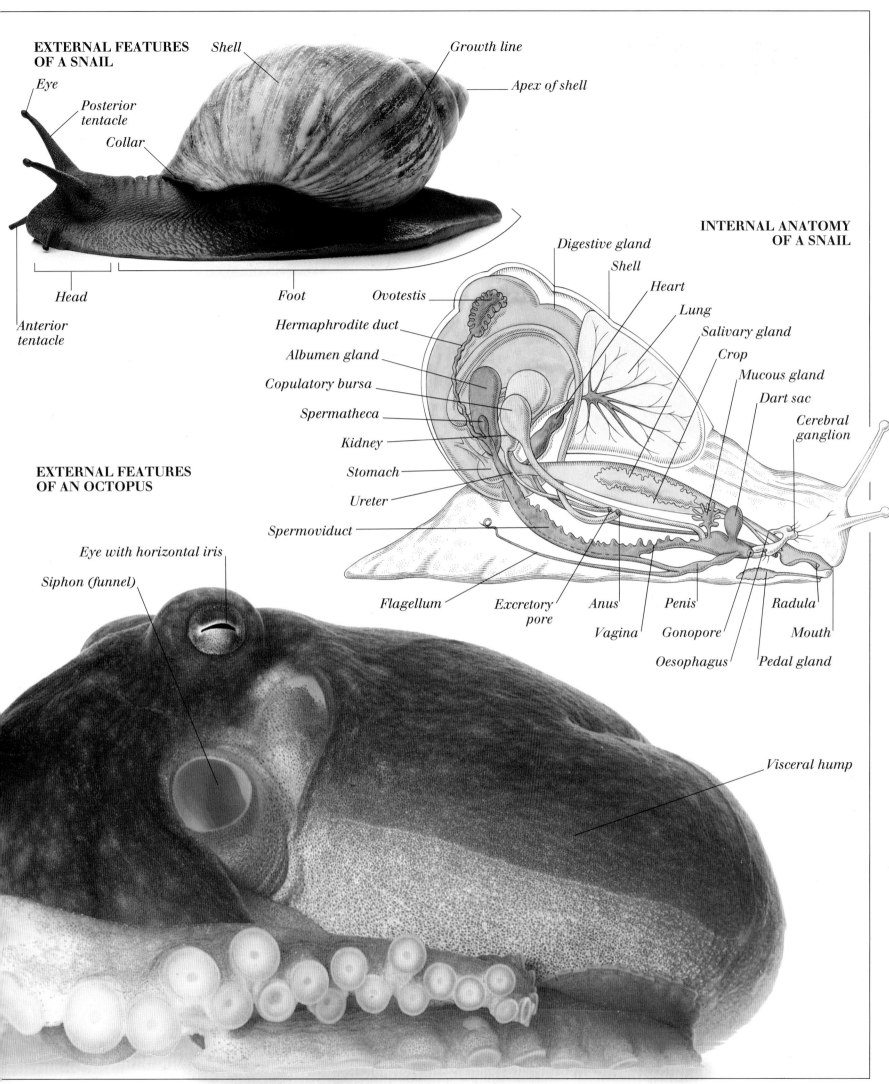

EXTERNAL FEATURES OF A SNAIL

Eye

Posterior tentacle

Collar

Shell

Growth line

Apex of shell

Head

Anterior tentacle

Foot

INTERNAL ANATOMY OF A SNAIL

Digestive gland

Shell

Heart

Lung

Salivary gland

Crop

Mucous gland

Dart sac

Cerebral ganglion

Ovotestis

Hermaphrodite duct

Albumen gland

Copulatory bursa

Spermatheca

Kidney

Stomach

Ureter

Spermoviduct

Flagellum

Excretory pore

Anus

Penis

Radula

Vagina

Gonopore

Mouth

Oesophagus

Pedal gland

EXTERNAL FEATURES OF AN OCTOPUS

Eye with horizontal iris

Siphon (funnel)

Visceral hump

Crustaceans

THE SUBPHYLUM CRUSTACEA is one of the largest groups in the phylum Arthropoda. The subphylum is divided into several classes, the most important of which are Malacostraca and Cirripedia. The class Malacostraca includes crayfish, crabs, lobsters, and shrimps. Typical features of malacostracans include a body divided into two sections (a combined head and thorax called a cephalothorax, and an abdomen); an exoskeleton (external skeleton) with a large plate (carapace) covering the cephalothorax; stalked, compound eyes; and two pairs of antennae. The class Cirripedia includes barnacles, which, unlike other crustaceans, spend their adult lives attached to a surface, such as a rock. Other characteristics of cirripedes include an exoskeleton of overlapping calcareous plates; a body consisting almost entirely of thorax (the abdomen and head are minute); and six pairs of thoracic appendages (cirri) used for filter feeding.

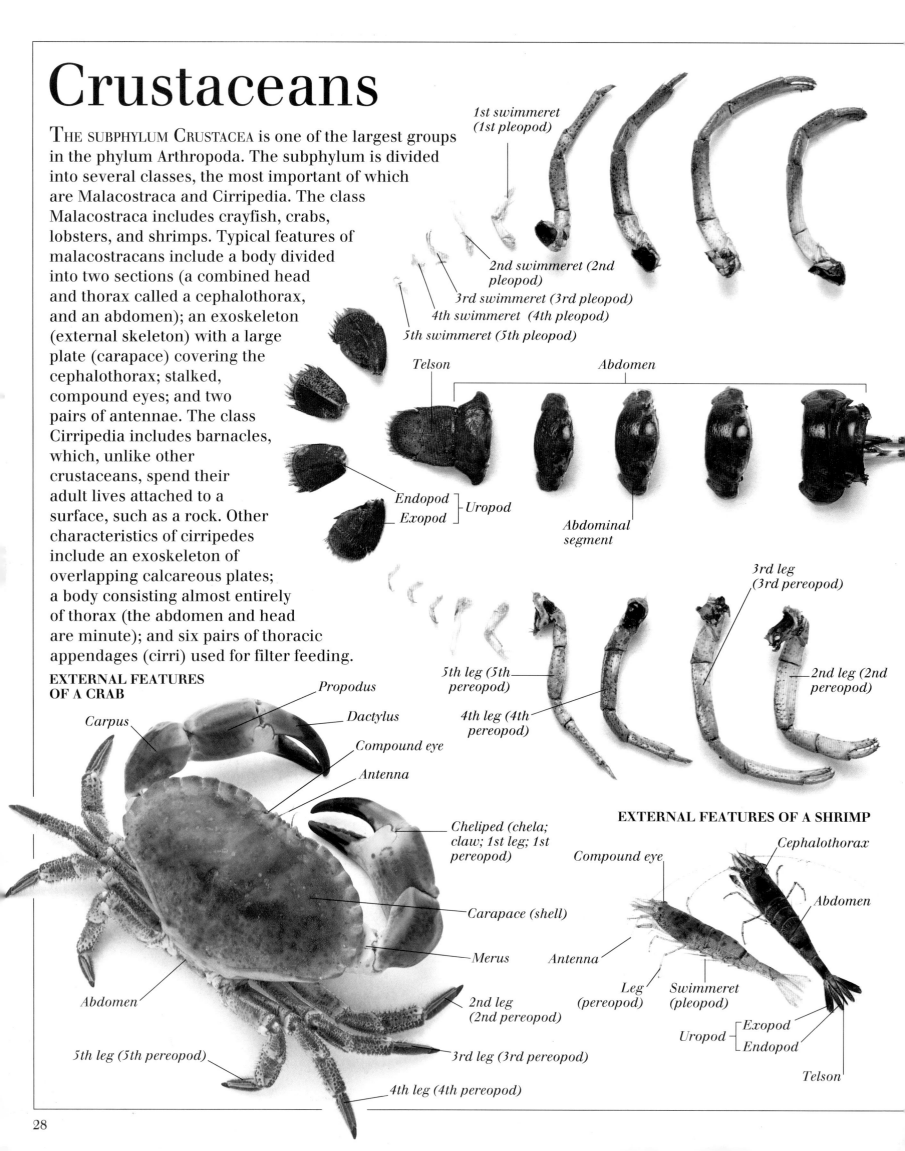

1st swimmeret (1st pleopod)

2nd swimmeret (2nd pleopod)

3rd swimmeret (3rd pleopod)

4th swimmeret (4th pleopod)

5th swimmeret (5th pleopod)

Telson

Abdomen

Endopod
Exopod ⎤ Uropod

Abdominal segment

3rd leg (3rd pereopod)

5th leg (5th pereopod)

4th leg (4th pereopod)

2nd leg (2nd pereopod)

EXTERNAL FEATURES OF A CRAB

Propodus

Carpus

Dactylus

Compound eye

Antenna

Cheliped (chela; claw; 1st leg; 1st pereopod)

Carapace (shell)

Merus

Abdomen

5th leg (5th pereopod)

3rd leg (3rd pereopod)

2nd leg (2nd pereopod)

4th leg (4th pereopod)

EXTERNAL FEATURES OF A SHRIMP

Compound eye

Cephalothorax

Abdomen

Antenna

Leg (pereopod)

Swimmeret (pleopod)

Uropod ⎱ Exopod
⎰ Endopod

Telson

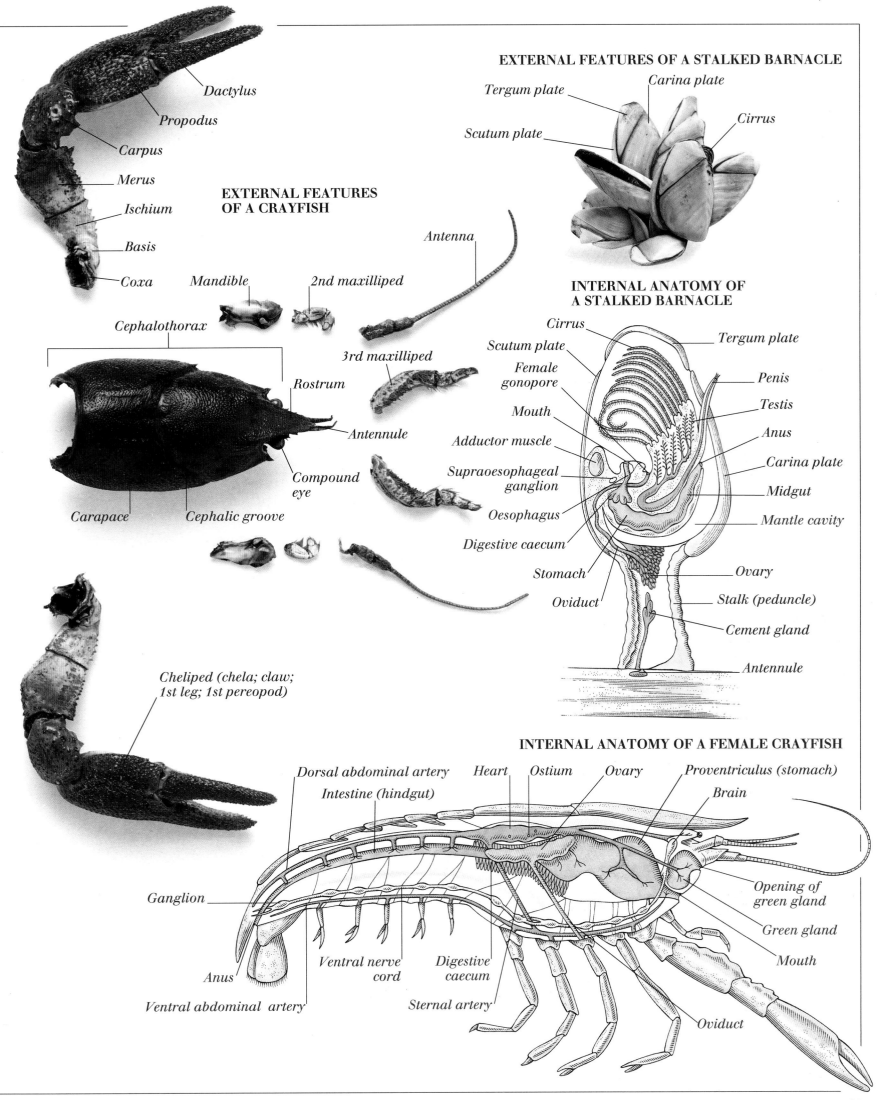

EXTERNAL FEATURES OF A STALKED BARNACLE

Tergum plate

Carina plate

Scutum plate

Cirrus

EXTERNAL FEATURES OF A CRAYFISH

Dactylus

Propodus

Carpus

Merus

Ischium

Basis

Coxa

Mandible

2nd maxilliped

Antenna

3rd maxilliped

Cephalothorax

Rostrum

Antennule

Compound eye

Carapace

Cephalic groove

INTERNAL ANATOMY OF A STALKED BARNACLE

Cirrus

Tergum plate

Scutum plate

Female gonopore

Penis

Testis

Mouth

Anus

Adductor muscle

Carina plate

Supraoesophageal ganglion

Midgut

Oesophagus

Mantle cavity

Digestive caecum

Stomach

Ovary

Oviduct

Stalk (peduncle)

Cement gland

Antennule

Cheliped (chela; claw; 1st leg; 1st pereopod)

INTERNAL ANATOMY OF A FEMALE CRAYFISH

Dorsal abdominal artery

Heart

Ostium

Ovary

Proventriculus (stomach)

Intestine (hindgut)

Brain

Ganglion

Opening of green gland

Green gland

Mouth

Anus

Ventral nerve cord

Digestive caecum

Oviduct

Ventral abdominal artery

Sternal artery

Amphibians

THE CLASS AMPHIBIA INCLUDES FROGS and toads (which make up the order Anura), and newts and salamanders (which make up the order Urodela). Amphibians typically have moist, scaleless, hairless skin; lungs; and are cold-blooded. They also undergo complete metamorphosis, from eggs laid in water through various water-living larval stages (such as tadpoles) to land-living adults. Typical features of adult frogs and toads include a squat body with no tail; long, powerful hind legs; and large, often bulging, eyes. Adult newts and salamanders typically have a long body with a well-developed tail; and relatively short, equal-sized legs. However, newts and salamanders show considerable variation; for example, in some species the adults have minute legs, external gills rather than lungs, and spend their entire lives in water.

INTERNAL ANATOMY OF A FEMALE FROG

EXTERNAL FEATURES OF A FROG

EXTERNAL FEATURES OF A SALAMANDER

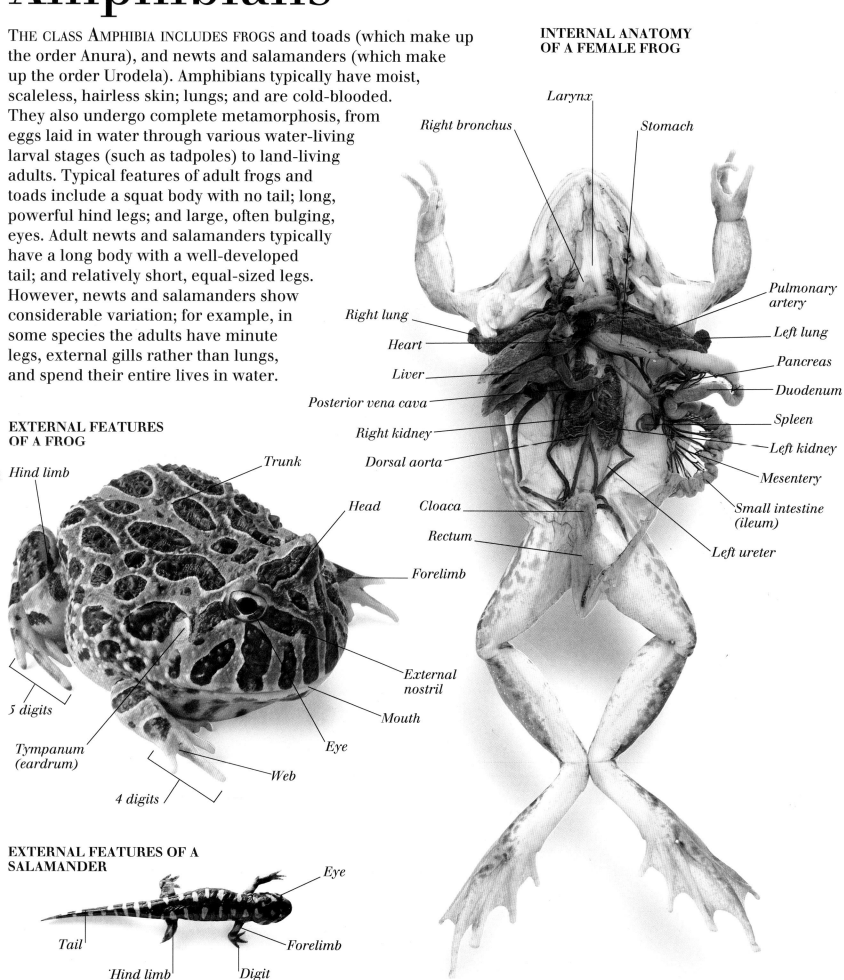

Larynx
Right bronchus
Stomach
Right lung
Pulmonary artery
Left lung
Heart
Liver
Pancreas
Posterior vena cava
Duodenum
Spleen
Right kidney
Left kidney
Dorsal aorta
Mesentery
Cloaca
Small intestine (ileum)
Rectum
Left ureter

Hind limb
Trunk
Head
Forelimb
5 digits
External nostril
Mouth
Tympanum (eardrum)
Eye
Web
4 digits

Eye
Tail
Forelimb
Hind limb
Digit

EGGS (SPAWN)

YOUNG TADPOLES

MATURE TADPOLE

YOUNG FROG

METAMORPHOSIS OF FROGS

Frogs undergo complete metamorphosis. Eggs (spawn) are laid in water and hatch into young tadpoles, which have a tail and external gills but no legs. As the tadpoles grow, the gills disappear, back legs develop, then front legs, and the tail shrinks. Eventually the tail disappears, resulting in a young adult frog.

SKELETON OF A FROG

Premaxilla

Sphenethmoid bone

Nasal bone

Maxilla

Frontoparietal bone

Pterygoid bone

Pro-otic bone

Quadratojugal bone

Phalanges

Squamosal bone

Exoccipital bone

Suprascapula

Carpals

Vertebra

Metacarpals

Radio-ulna

Phalanges

Humerus

Metatarsal

Sacral vertebra

Ilium

Distal tarsals

Femur

Astragalus (tibiale)

Proximal tarsals

Urostyle

Calcaneum (fibulare)

Tibiofibula

Ischium

Lizards and snakes

LIZARDS AND SNAKES BELONG to the order Squamata, a division of the class Reptilia. Characteristic reptilian features include scaly skin, lungs, and cold-bloodedness. Most reptiles lay leathery-shelled eggs, although some hatch the eggs inside their bodies and give birth to live young. Lizards belong to the suborder Lacertilia. Typically, they have long tails, and shed their skin in several pieces. Many lizards can regenerate a tail if it is lost; some can change colour; and some are limbless. Snakes make up the suborder Ophidia (also called Serpentes). All snakes have long, limbless bodies; can dislocate their lower jaw to swallow large prey; and have eyelids that are joined together to form a single transparent covering over the front of the eye. Most snakes shed their skin in a single piece. Constrictor snakes kill their prey by squeezing; venomous snakes poison their prey.

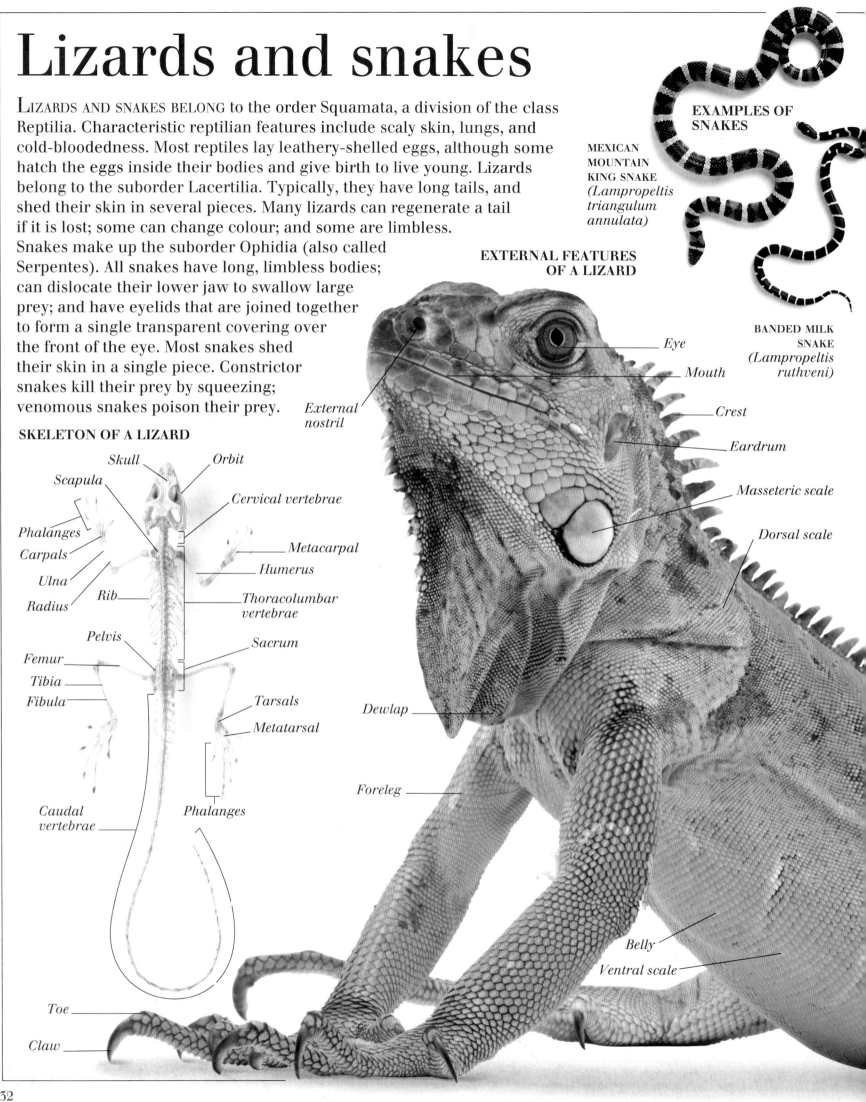

EXAMPLES OF SNAKES

MEXICAN MOUNTAIN KING SNAKE
(*Lampropeltis triangulum annulata*)

BANDED MILK SNAKE
(*Lampropeltis ruthveni*)

EXTERNAL FEATURES OF A LIZARD

Eye

Mouth

Crest

Eardrum

Masseteric scale

Dorsal scale

External nostril

Dewlap

Foreleg

Belly

Ventral scale

SKELETON OF A LIZARD

Skull

Orbit

Scapula

Cervical vertebrae

Phalanges

Carpals

Metacarpal

Humerus

Ulna

Radius

Rib

Thoracolumbar vertebrae

Pelvis

Sacrum

Femur

Tibia

Fibula

Tarsals

Metatarsal

Caudal vertebrae

Phalanges

Toe

Claw

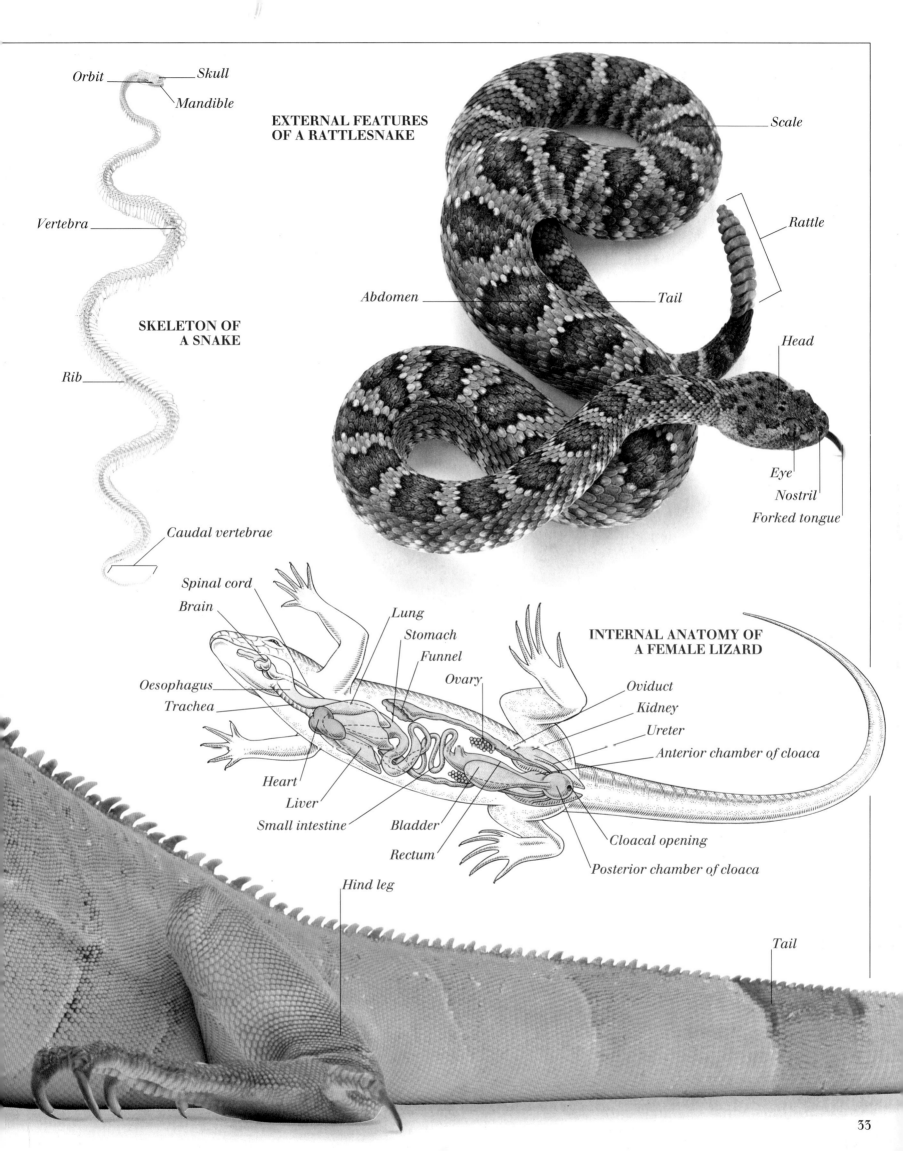

Orbit — Skull

Mandible

EXTERNAL FEATURES OF A RATTLESNAKE

Scale

Vertebra

Rattle

Abdomen — Tail

SKELETON OF A SNAKE

Head

Rib

Eye

Nostril

Forked tongue

Caudal vertebrae

Spinal cord

Brain

Lung

Stomach

INTERNAL ANATOMY OF A FEMALE LIZARD

Funnel

Ovary

Oesophagus

Oviduct

Trachea

Kidney

Ureter

Anterior chamber of cloaca

Heart

Liver

Bladder

Small intestine

Cloacal opening

Rectum

Posterior chamber of cloaca

Hind leg

Tail

Crocodilians and turtles

CROCODILIANS AND TURTLES BELONG to different orders in the class Reptilia. The order Crocodilia includes crocodiles, alligators, caimans, and gharials. Typically, crocodilians are carnivores (flesh-eaters), and have a long snout, sharp teeth for gripping prey, and hard, square scales. All crocodilians are a lapted to living on land and in water: they have four strong legs for moving on land; a powerful tail for swimming; and their eyes and nostrils are high on the head so that they stay above water while the rest of the body is submerged. The order Chelonia includes marine turtles, terrapins (freshwater turtles), and tortoises (land turtles). Characteristically, chelonians have a short, broad body encased in a bony shell with an outer horny covering, into which the head and limbs can be withdrawn; and a horny beak instead of teeth.

SKULLS OF CROCODILIANS

GHARIAL
(Gavialis gangeticus)

NILE CROCODILE
(Crocodylus niloticus)

AMERICAN ALLIGATOR
(Alligator mississippiensis)

SKELETON OF A CROCODILE

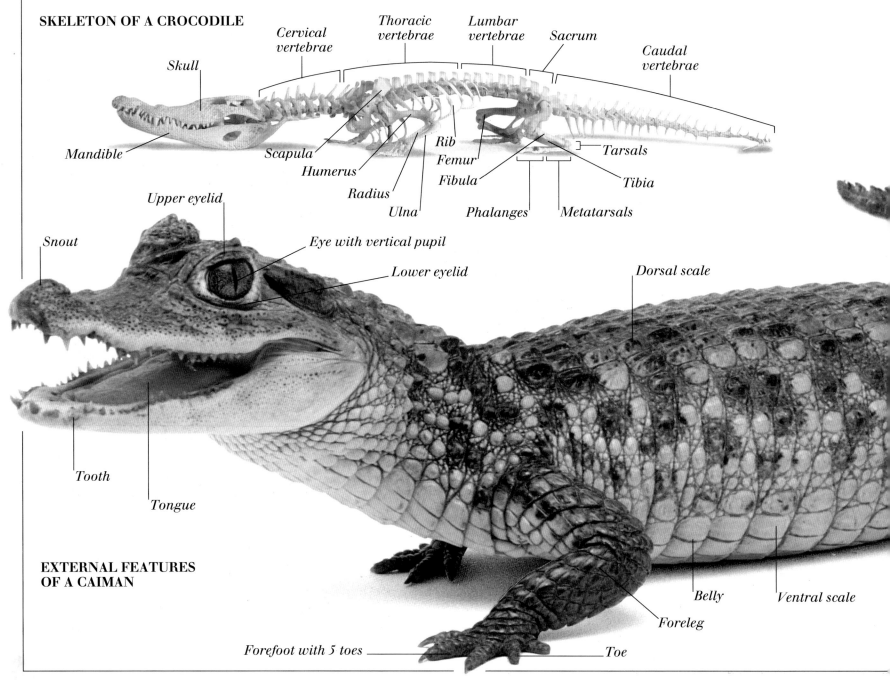

Skull

Mandible

Cervical vertebrae

Thoracic vertebrae

Lumbar vertebrae

Sacrum

Caudal vertebrae

Scapula

Humerus

Radius

Ulna

Rib

Femur

Fibula

Phalanges

Metatarsals

Tarsals

Tibia

Upper eyelid

Eye with vertical pupil

Lower eyelid

Dorsal scale

Snout

Tooth

Tongue

EXTERNAL FEATURES OF A CAIMAN

Belly

Ventral scale

Foreleg

Forefoot with 5 toes

Toe

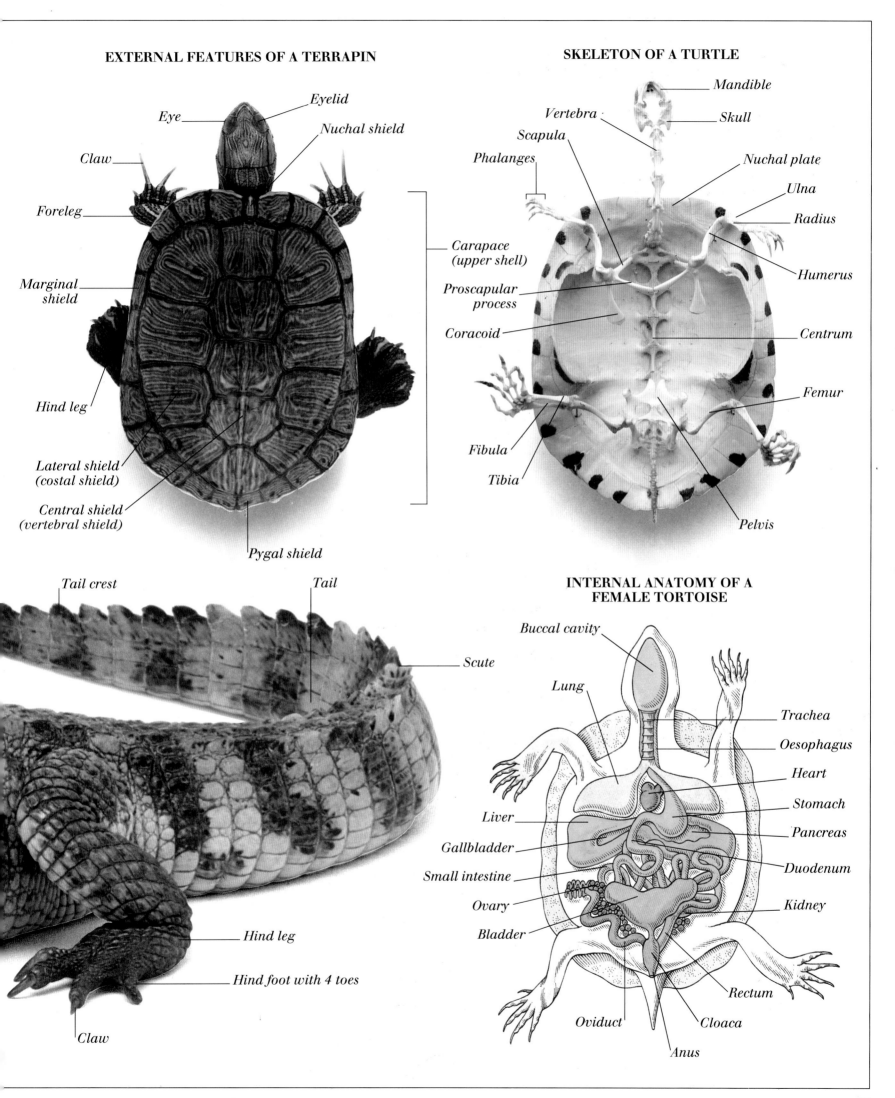

EXTERNAL FEATURES OF A TERRAPIN

Eye
Eyelid
Nuchal shield
Claw
Foreleg
Marginal shield
Carapace (upper shell)
Hind leg
Lateral shield (costal shield)
Central shield (vertebral shield)
Pygal shield

Tail crest
Tail
Scute
Hind leg
Hind foot with 4 toes
Claw

SKELETON OF A TURTLE

Mandible
Vertebra
Skull
Scapula
Phalanges
Nuchal plate
Ulna
Radius
Proscapular process
Humerus
Coracoid
Centrum
Femur
Fibula
Tibia
Pelvis

INTERNAL ANATOMY OF A FEMALE TORTOISE

Buccal cavity
Lung
Trachea
Oesophagus
Heart
Liver
Stomach
Pancreas
Gallbladder
Duodenum
Small intestine
Ovary
Kidney
Bladder
Rectum
Oviduct
Cloaca
Anus

Birds 1

BIRDS MAKE UP THE CLASS AVES. There are more than 9,000 species, almost all of which can fly (the only flightless birds are penguins, ostriches, rheas, cassowaries, and kiwis). The ability to fly is reflected in the typical bird features: forelimbs modified as wings; a streamlined body; and hollow bones to reduce weight. All birds lay hard-shelled eggs, which the parents incubate. Birds' beaks and feet vary according to diet and way of life. Beaks range from general-purpose types suitable for a mixed diet (those of thrushes, for example), to types specialized for particular foods (such as the large, curved, sieving beaks of flamingos). Feet range from the webbed "paddles" of ducks, to the talons of birds of prey. Plumage also varies widely, and in many species the male is brightly coloured for courtship display whereas the female is drab.

EXTERNAL FEATURES OF A BIRD

Forehead

Eye

Crown

Nostril

Nape

Upper mandible

Beak

Lower mandible

Chin

Throat

EXAMPLES OF BIRDS

MALE TUFTED DUCK
(*Aythya fuligula*)

WHITE STORK
(*Ciconia ciconia*)

MALE OSTRICH
(*Struthio camelus*)

Minor coverts

Lesser wing coverts

Median wing coverts

Greater wing coverts
(major coverts)

Secondary flight feathers
(secondary remiges)

Primary flight feathers
(primary remiges)

Breast

Belly

Flank

Thigh

Under tail coverts

Claw

Tarsus

Toe

Tail feathers (retrices)

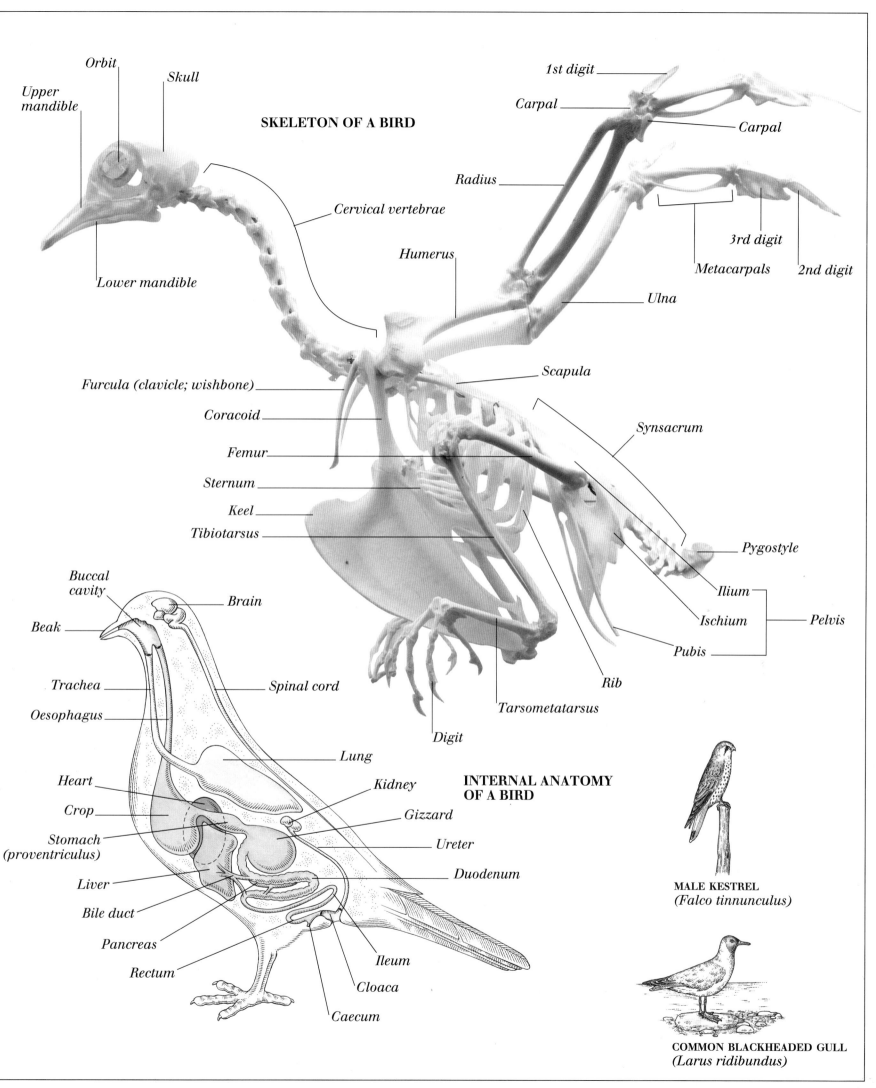

SKELETON OF A BIRD

Orbit

Skull

Upper mandible

1st digit

Carpal

Carpal

Radius

Cervical vertebrae

Humerus

3rd digit

Metacarpals

2nd digit

Lower mandible

Ulna

Scapula

Furcula (clavicle; wishbone)

Coracoid

Synsacrum

Femur

Sternum

Keel

Tibiotarsus

Pygostyle

Ilium

Ischium

Pelvis

Pubis

Rib

Tarsometatarsus

Buccal cavity

Brain

Beak

Spinal cord

Trachea

Oesophagus

Digit

Lung

INTERNAL ANATOMY OF A BIRD

Heart

Kidney

Crop

Gizzard

Stomach (proventriculus)

Ureter

Duodenum

Liver

Bile duct

Pancreas

Ileum

Rectum

Cloaca

Caecum

MALE KESTREL (Falco tinnunculus)

COMMON BLACKHEADED GULL (Larus ridibundus)

37

Birds 2

EXAMPLES OF BIRDS' FEET

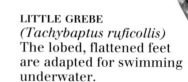

KITTIWAKE
(Rissa tridactyla)
The webbed feet are
adapted for paddling
through water.

LITTLE GREBE
(Tachybaptus ruficollis)
The lobed, flattened feet
are adapted for swimming
underwater.

TAWNY OWL
(Strix aluco)
The clawed feet are adapted
for gripping prey.

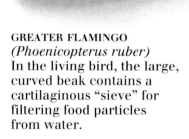

EXAMPLES OF BIRDS' BEAKS

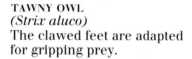

KING VULTURE
(Sarcorhamphus papa)
The hooked beak is adapted
for pulling apart flesh.

GREATER FLAMINGO
(Phoenicopterus ruber)
In the living bird, the large,
curved beak contains a
cartilaginous "sieve" for
filtering food particles
from water.

MISTLE THRUSH
(Turdus viscivorus)
The general-purpose beak is
suitable for a wide range of animal
and plant foods.

BLUE-AND-YELLOW MACAW
(Ara ararauna)
The broad, powerful, hooked beak
is adapted for crushing seeds and
eating fruit.

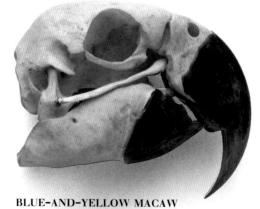

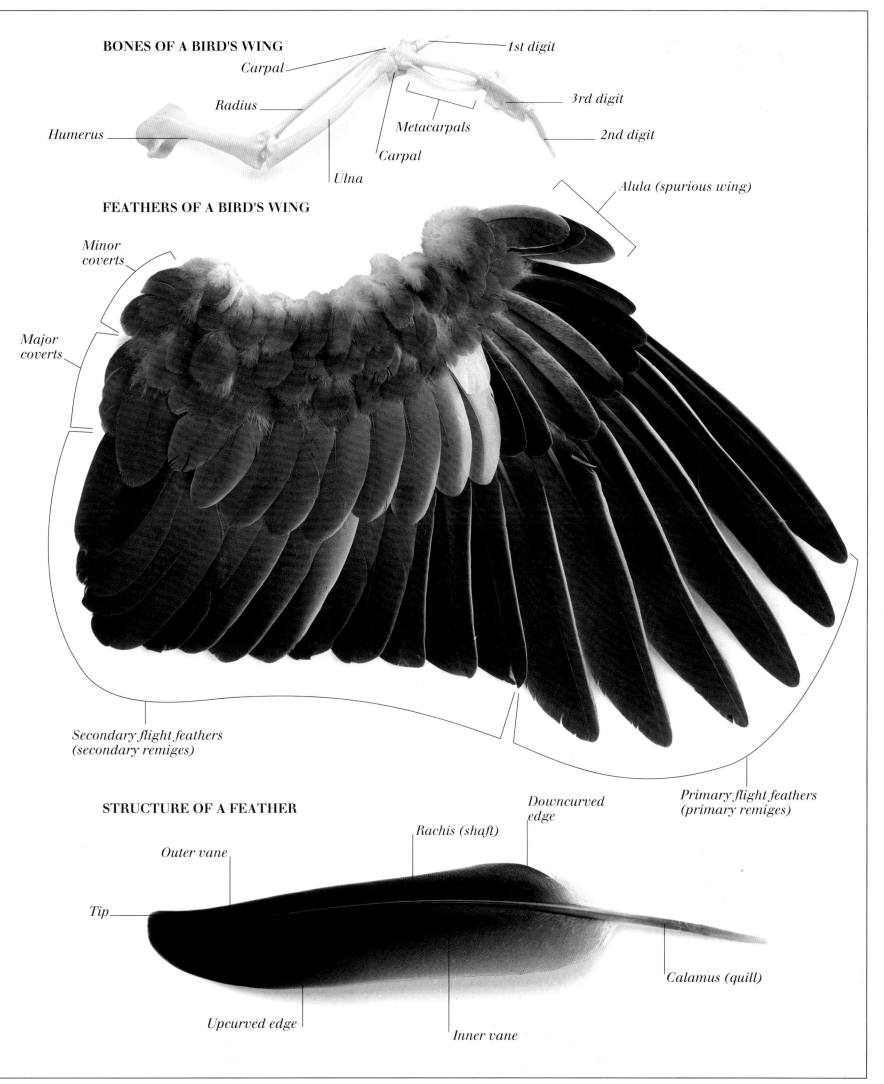

BONES OF A BIRD'S WING

1st digit

Carpal

Radius

3rd digit

Humerus

Metacarpals

Carpal

2nd digit

Ulna

Alula (spurious wing)

FEATHERS OF A BIRD'S WING

Minor coverts

Major coverts

Secondary flight feathers (secondary remiges)

Primary flight feathers (primary remiges)

STRUCTURE OF A FEATHER

Downcurved edge

Rachis (shaft)

Outer vane

Tip

Calamus (quill)

Upcurved edge

Inner vane

Eggs

AN EGG IS A SINGLE CELL, produced by the female, with the capacity to develop into a new individual. Development may take place inside the mother's body (as in most mammals) or outside, in which case the egg has a protective covering such as a shell. Egg yolk nourishes the growing young. Eggs developing inside the mother generally have little yolk, because the young are nourished from her body. Eggs developing outside may also have little yolk if they are produced by animals whose young go through a larval stage (such as a caterpillar) that feeds itself while developing into the adult form. The shelled eggs of birds and reptiles contain enough yolk to sustain the young until it hatches into a juvenile version of the adult.

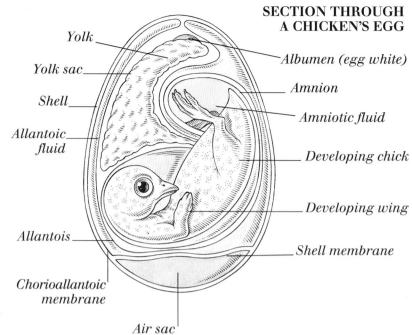

SECTION THROUGH A CHICKEN'S EGG

Yolk
Yolk sac
Shell
Allantoic fluid
Allantois
Chorioallantoic membrane
Air sac
Albumen (egg white)
Amnion
Amniotic fluid
Developing chick
Developing wing
Shell membrane

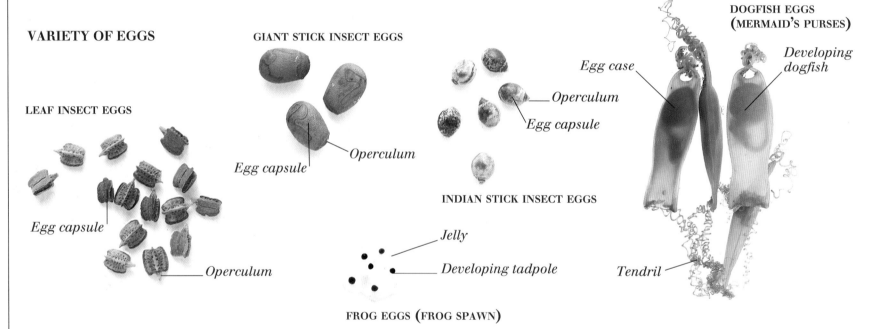

VARIETY OF EGGS

GIANT STICK INSECT EGGS

LEAF INSECT EGGS

Egg capsule
Operculum

Egg capsule
Operculum

INDIAN STICK INSECT EGGS

Operculum
Egg capsule

DOGFISH EGGS (MERMAID'S PURSES)

Egg case
Developing dogfish
Tendril

Jelly
Developing tadpole

FROG EGGS (FROG SPAWN)

HATCHING OF A QUAIL'S EGG

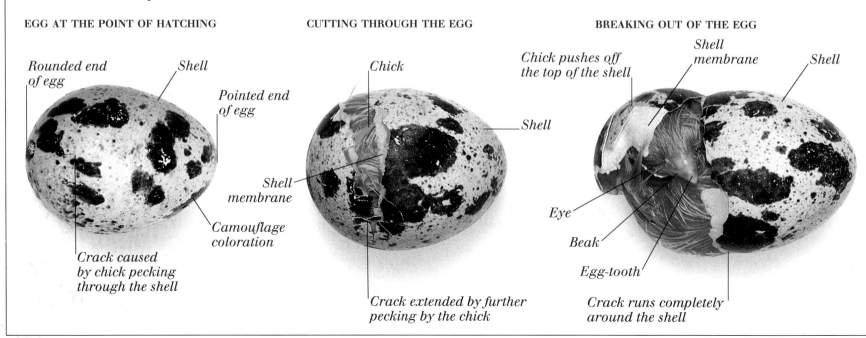

EGG AT THE POINT OF HATCHING

Rounded end of egg
Shell
Pointed end of egg
Camouflage coloration
Crack caused by chick pecking through the shell

CUTTING THROUGH THE EGG

Chick
Shell
Shell membrane
Crack extended by further pecking by the chick

BREAKING OUT OF THE EGG

Chick pushes off the top of the shell
Shell membrane
Shell
Eye
Beak
Egg-tooth
Crack runs completely around the shell

EXAMPLES OF BIRDS' EGGS

BEE HUMMINGBIRD
(Calypte helenae)

GREATER BLACKBACKED GULL
(Larus marinus)

BALTIMORE ORIOLE
(Icterus galbula)

WILLOW GROUSE
(Lagopus lagopus)

COMMON TERN
(Sterna hirundo)

CARRION CROW
(Corvus corone)

CHAFFINCH
(Fringilla coelebs)

OSTRICH
(Struthio camelus)

EMERGING FROM THE EGG

Eye

Beak

Egg-tooth

Chick heaves itself out of the egg

Tympanum (eardrum)

Shell

Wet down

Remains of egg membranes (amnion and allantois)

THE NEWLY HATCHED CHICK

Eye

Beak

Egg-tooth

Nostril

Tympanum (eardrum)

Chick is dry about an hour after hatching

Dry down

Toe

Claw

Leg

Eggshell

41

Carnivores

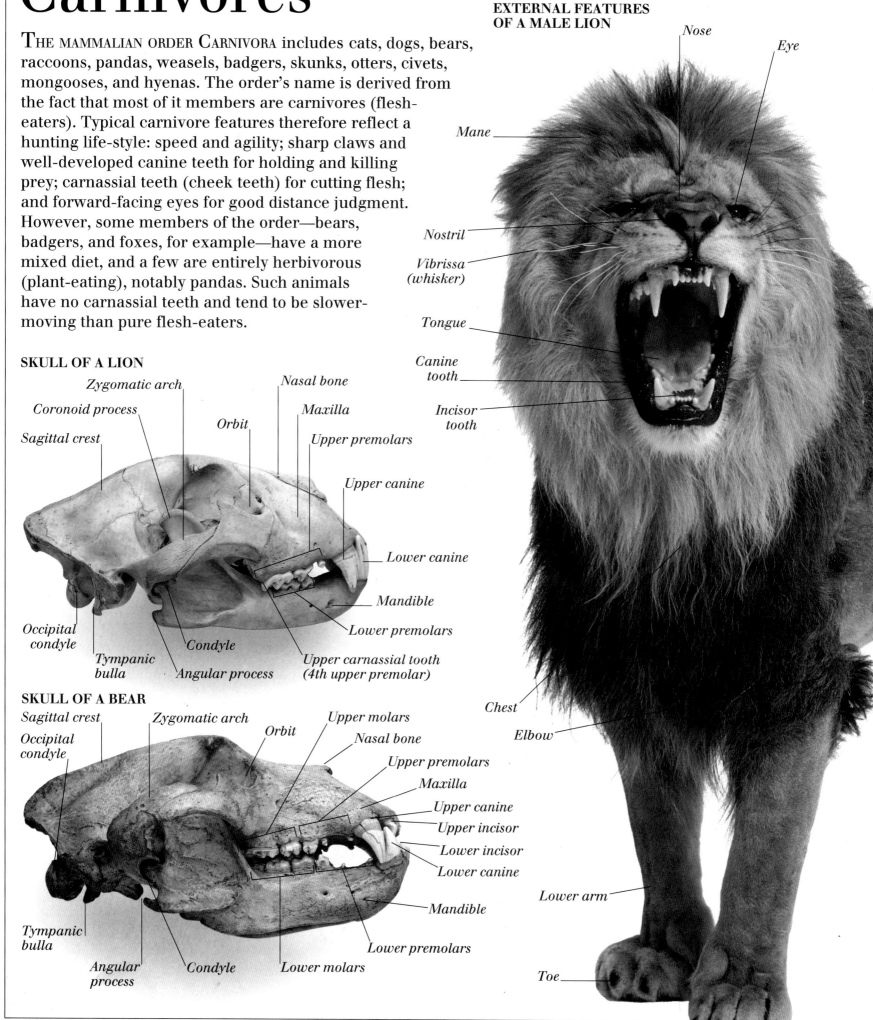

THE MAMMALIAN ORDER CARNIVORA includes cats, dogs, bears, raccoons, pandas, weasels, badgers, skunks, otters, civets, mongooses, and hyenas. The order's name is derived from the fact that most of it members are carnivores (flesh-eaters). Typical carnivore features therefore reflect a hunting life-style: speed and agility; sharp claws and well-developed canine teeth for holding and killing prey; carnassial teeth (cheek teeth) for cutting flesh; and forward-facing eyes for good distance judgment. However, some members of the order—bears, badgers, and foxes, for example—have a more mixed diet, and a few are entirely herbivorous (plant-eating), notably pandas. Such animals have no carnassial teeth and tend to be slower-moving than pure flesh-eaters.

EXTERNAL FEATURES OF A MALE LION

Nose

Eye

Mane

Nostril

Vibrissa (whisker)

Tongue

Canine tooth

Incisor tooth

Chest

Elbow

Lower arm

Toe

SKULL OF A LION

Zygomatic arch

Coronoid process

Nasal bone

Sagittal crest

Orbit

Maxilla

Upper premolars

Upper canine

Lower canine

Mandible

Occipital condyle

Lower premolars

Tympanic bulla

Condyle

Upper carnassial tooth (4th upper premolar)

Angular process

SKULL OF A BEAR

Sagittal crest

Zygomatic arch

Upper molars

Orbit

Occipital condyle

Nasal bone

Upper premolars

Maxilla

Upper canine

Upper incisor

Lower incisor

Lower canine

Mandible

Tympanic bulla

Lower premolars

Angular process

Condyle

Lower molars

EXAMPLES OF CARNIVORES

ALSATIAN DOG
(Canis familiaris)

MANED WOLF
(Chrysocyon brachyurus)

RACCOON
(Procyon lotor)

AMERICAN BLACK BEAR
(Ursus americanus)

SKELETON OF A DOMESTIC CAT

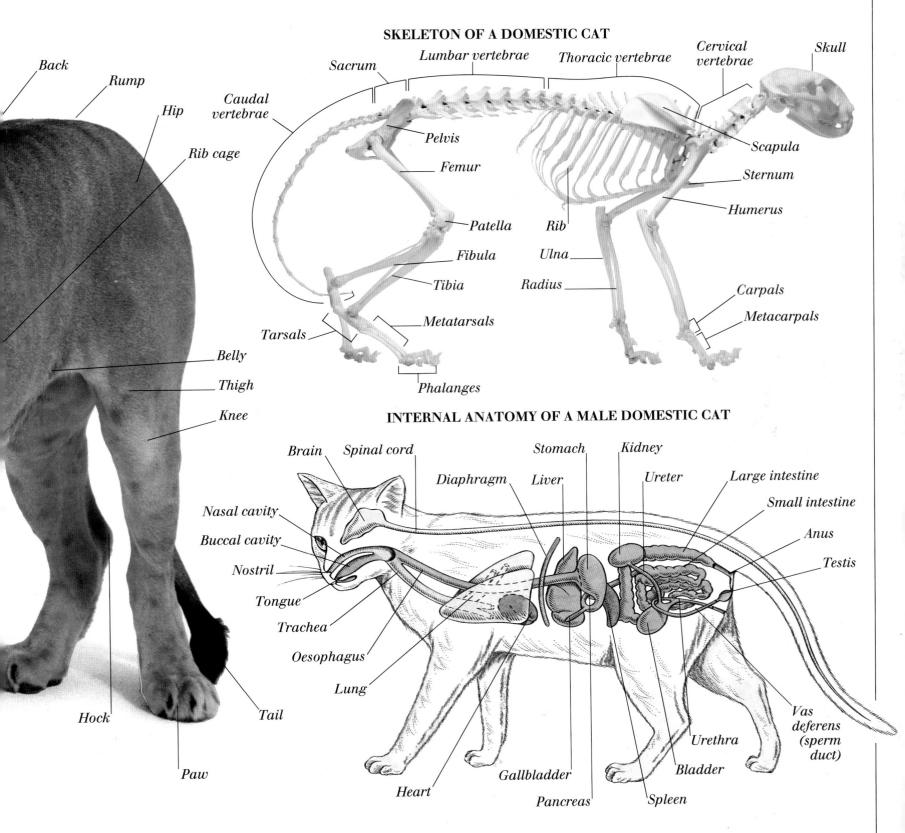

Back
Rump
Hip
Rib cage
Caudal vertebrae
Sacrum
Lumbar vertebrae
Thoracic vertebrae
Cervical vertebrae
Skull
Pelvis
Scapula
Femur
Sternum
Humerus
Patella
Rib
Ulna
Fibula
Radius
Tibia
Carpals
Metacarpals
Metatarsals
Tarsals
Belly
Thigh
Knee
Phalanges

INTERNAL ANATOMY OF A MALE DOMESTIC CAT

Brain
Spinal cord
Stomach
Kidney
Diaphragm
Liver
Ureter
Large intestine
Small intestine
Nasal cavity
Anus
Buccal cavity
Testis
Nostril
Tongue
Trachea
Oesophagus
Lung
Vas deferens (sperm duct)
Hock
Tail
Urethra
Paw
Bladder
Heart
Gallbladder
Pancreas
Spleen

Rabbits and rodents

ALTHOUGH RABBITS AND RODENTS belong to different orders of mammals, they have some features in common. These features include chisel-shaped incisor teeth that grow continually, and eating their faeces to extract more nutrients from their plant diet. Rabbits and hares belong to the order Lagomorpha. Characteristically, they have four incisors in the upper jaw and two in the lower jaw; powerful hind legs for jumping; forelimbs adapted for burrowing; long ears; and a small tail. Rodents make up the order Rodentia. This is the largest order of mammals, with more than 1,700 species, including squirrels, beavers, chipmunks, gophers, rats, mice, lemmings, gerbils, porcupines, cavies, and the capybara. Typical rodent features include two incisors in each jaw; short forelimbs for manipulating food; and cheek pouches for storing food.

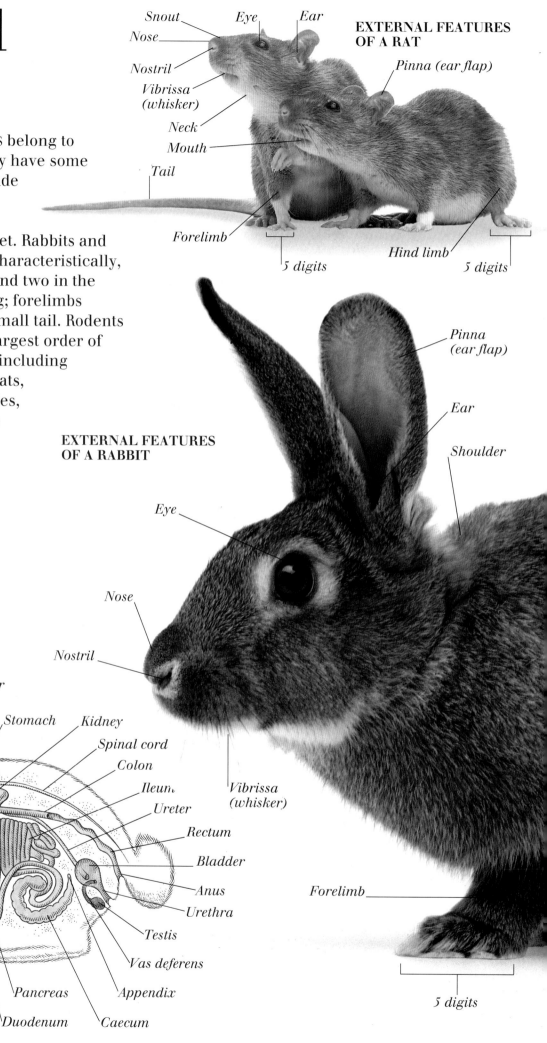

EXTERNAL FEATURES OF A RAT

Snout
Eye
Ear
Pinna (ear flap)
Nose
Nostril
Vibrissa (whisker)
Neck
Mouth
Tail
Forelimb
Hind limb
5 digits
5 digits

EXTERNAL FEATURES OF A RABBIT

Pinna (ear flap)
Ear
Shoulder
Eye
Nose
Nostril
Vibrissa (whisker)
Forelimb
5 digits

INTERNAL ANATOMY OF A MALE RABBIT

Brain
Gallbladder
Liver
Stomach
Kidney
Spinal cord
Colon
Ileum
Ureter
Rectum
Bladder
Anus
Urethra
Testis
Vas deferens
Appendix
Caecum
Duodenum
Pancreas
Heart
Diaphragm
Lung
Trachea
Oesophagus
Tongue
Buccal cavity
Mouth
Nasal cavity

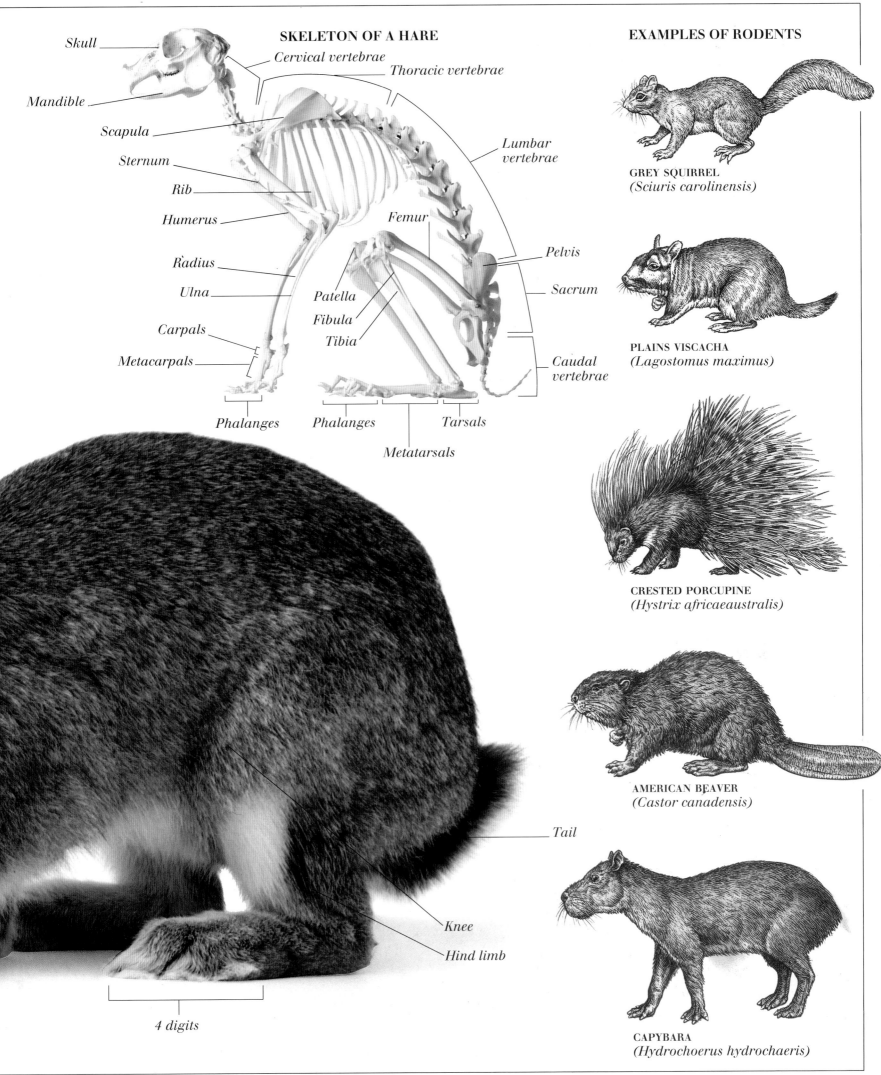

SKELETON OF A HARE

Skull

Mandible

Cervical vertebrae

Thoracic vertebrae

Scapula

Sternum

Rib

Humerus

Femur

Lumbar vertebrae

Radius

Patella

Pelvis

Ulna

Fibula

Sacrum

Tibia

Carpals

Caudal vertebrae

Metacarpals

Phalanges

Phalanges

Tarsals

Metatarsals

Tail

Knee

Hind limb

4 digits

EXAMPLES OF RODENTS

GREY SQUIRREL
(*Sciuris carolinensis*)

PLAINS VISCACHA
(*Lagostomus maximus*)

CRESTED PORCUPINE
(*Hystrix africaeaustralis*)

AMERICAN BEAVER
(*Castor canadensis*)

CAPYBARA
(*Hydrochoerus hydrochaeris*)

Ungulates

UNGULATES IS A GENERAL TERM FOR a large, varied group of mammals that includes horses, cattle, and their relatives. The ungulates are divided into two orders on the basis of the number of toes. Members of the order Perissodactyla (odd-toed ungulates) have one or three toes. Perissodactyls include horses, asses, and zebras (all of which are one-toed), and rhinoceroses and tapirs (which are three-toed). Members of the order Artiodactyla (even-toed ungulates) have two or four toes. Most artiodactyls have two toes, which are typically encased in hooves to give the so-called cloven hoof. Two-toed, cloven-hoofed artiodactyls include cows and other cattle, sheep, goats, antelopes, deer, and giraffes. The other main two-toed artiodactyls are camels and llamas. Most two-toed artiodactyls are ruminants; that is, they have a four-chambered stomach and chew the cud. The principal four-toed artiodactyls are pigs, peccaries, and hippopotamuses.

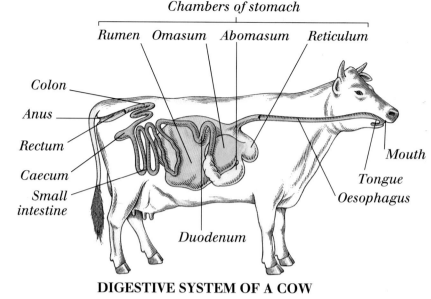

DIGESTIVE SYSTEM OF A COW

COMPARISON OF THE FRONT FEET OF A HORSE AND A COW

SKELETON OF THE LEFT FRONT FOOT OF A HORSE

SKELETON OF THE RIGHT FRONT FOOT OF A COW

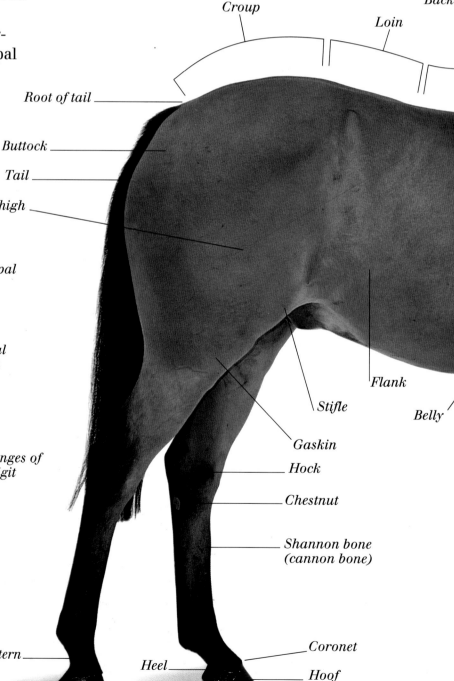

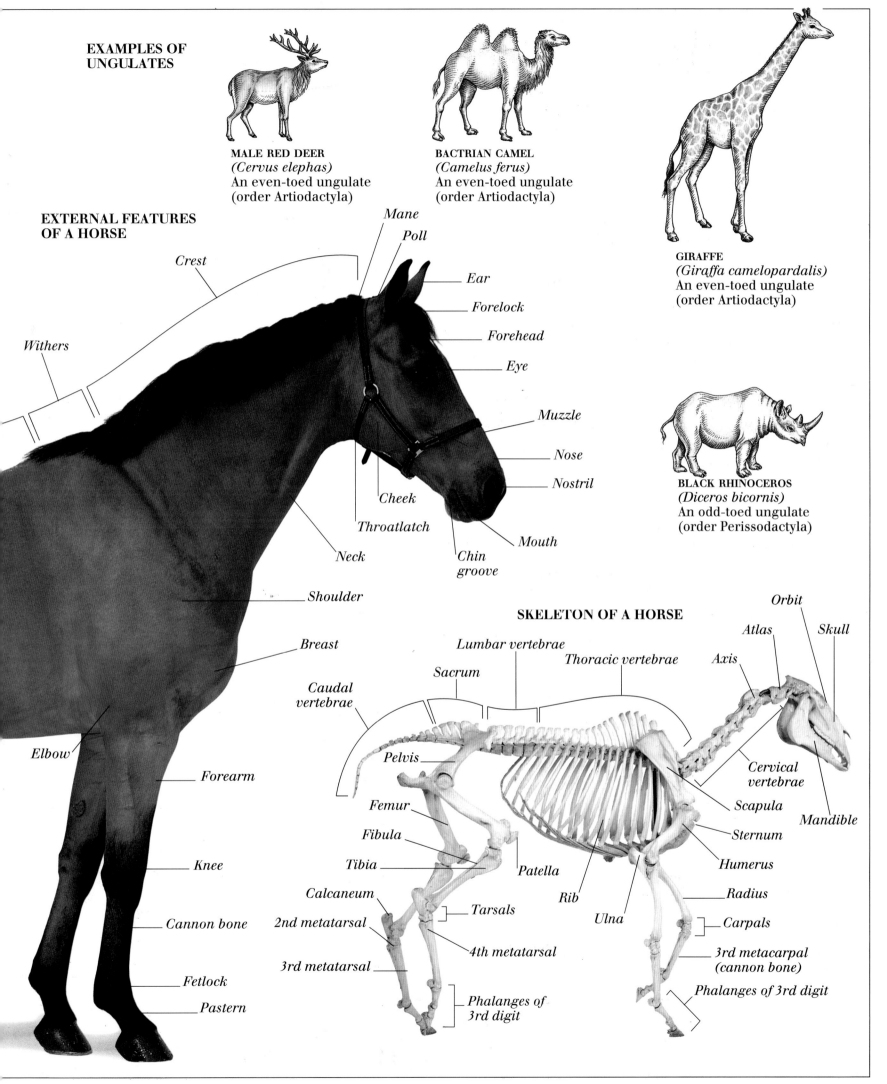

EXAMPLES OF
UNGULATES

MALE RED DEER
(Cervus elephas)
An even-toed ungulate
(order Artiodactyla)

BACTRIAN CAMEL
(Camelus ferus)
An even-toed ungulate
(order Artiodactyla)

GIRAFFE
(Giraffa camelopardalis)
An even-toed ungulate
(order Artiodactyla)

BLACK RHINOCEROS
(Diceros bicornis)
An odd-toed ungulate
(order Perissodactyla)

EXTERNAL FEATURES
OF A HORSE

Mane

Poll

Ear

Forelock

Forehead

Eye

Muzzle

Nose

Nostril

Crest

Withers

Cheek

Throatlatch

Neck

Chin groove

Mouth

Shoulder

Breast

Elbow

Forearm

Knee

Cannon bone

Fetlock

Pastern

SKELETON OF A HORSE

Orbit

Atlas

Skull

Axis

Lumbar vertebrae

Thoracic vertebrae

Sacrum

Caudal vertebrae

Pelvis

Cervical vertebrae

Scapula

Mandible

Femur

Sternum

Fibula

Humerus

Tibia

Patella

Calcaneum

Rib

Radius

2nd metatarsal

Tarsals

Ulna

Carpals

4th metatarsal

3rd metatarsal

3rd metacarpal (cannon bone)

Phalanges of 3rd digit

Phalanges of 3rd digit

Elephants

THE TWO SPECIES of elephants—African and Asian—are the only members of the mammalian order Proboscidea. The bigger African elephant is the largest land animal: a fully grown male may be up to 4 m (13 ft) tall and weigh as much as 7 tonnes (6.9 tons). A fully grown male Asian elephant may be 3.3 m (11 ft) tall and weigh 5.4 tonnes (5.3 tons). The trunk—an extension of the nose and upper lip—is the elephant's other most obvious feature It is used for manipulating and lifting, feeding, drinking and spraying water, smelling, touching, and producing trumpeting sounds. Other characteristic features include a pair of tusks, used for defence and for crushing vegetation; thick, pillar-like legs and broad feet to support the massive body; and large ear flaps that act as radiators to keep the elephant cool.

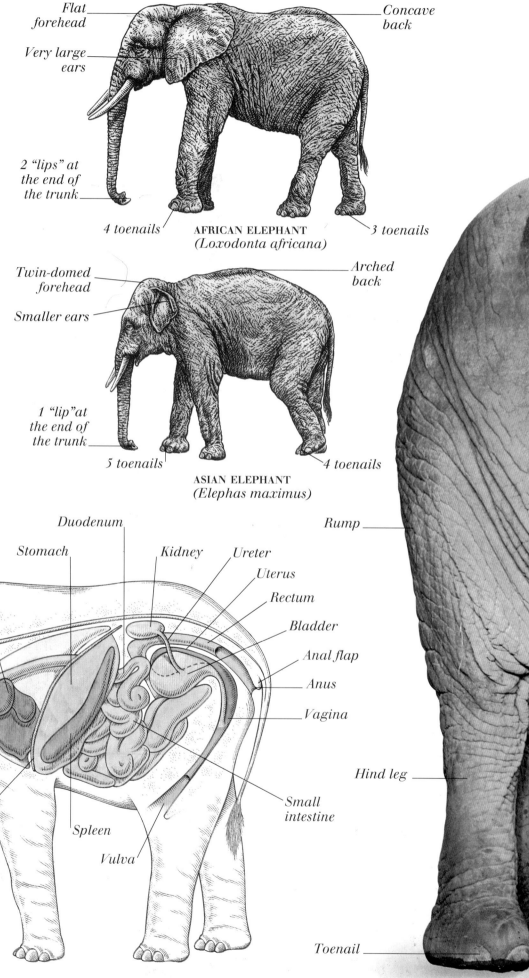

DIFFERENCES BETWEEN AFRICAN AND ASIAN ELEPHANTS

Flat forehead
Concave back
Very large ears
2 "lips" at the end of the trunk
4 toenails
AFRICAN ELEPHANT
(*Loxodonta africana*)
3 toenails

Twin-domed forehead
Arched back
Smaller ears
1 "lip" at the end of the trunk
5 toenails
4 toenails
ASIAN ELEPHANT
(*Elephas maximus*)

Rump
Hind leg
Toenail

INTERNAL ANATOMY OF A FEMALE ELEPHANT

Duodenum
Spinal cord
Heart
Stomach
Kidney
Ureter
Uterus
Rectum
Bladder
Brain
Anal flap
Nasal cavity
Anus
Buccal cavity
Vagina
Mouth
Tongue
Tusk
Epiglottis
Oesophagus
Trachea
Small intestine
Spleen
Lung
Vulva
Nasal passage
Diaphragm
Nostril

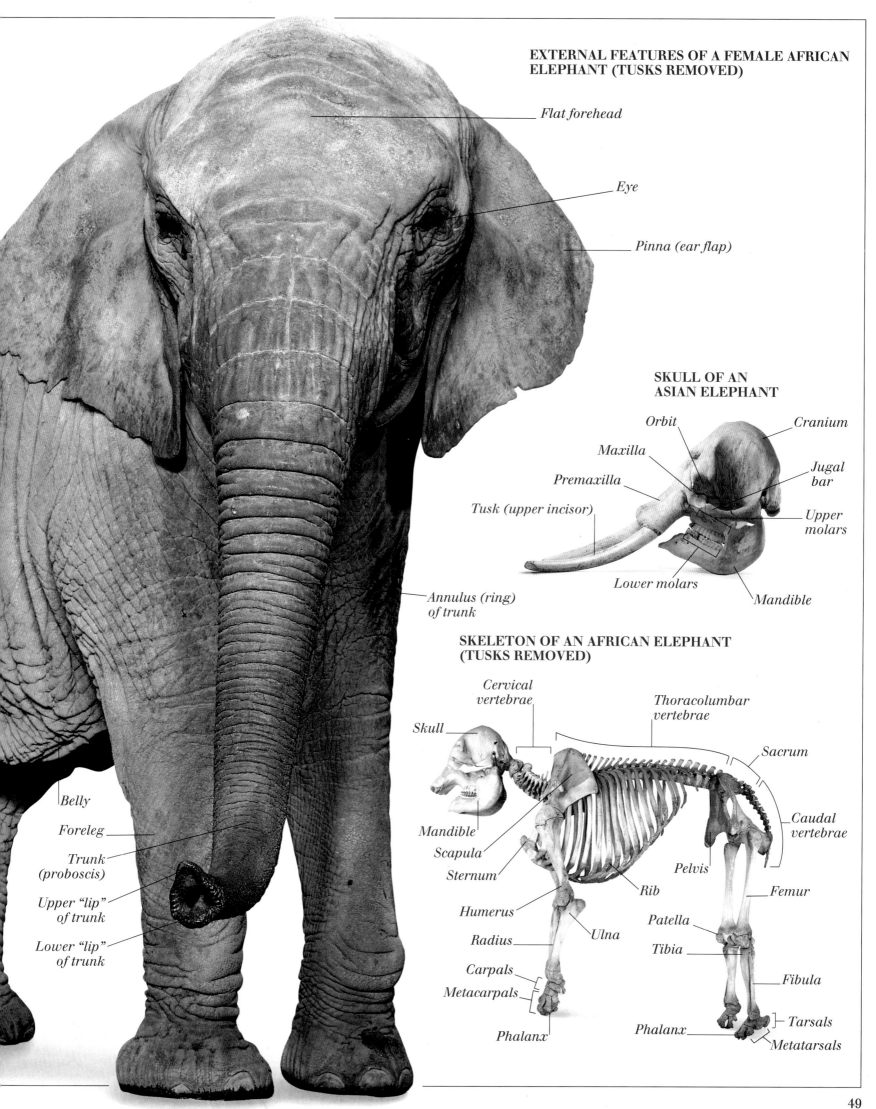

EXTERNAL FEATURES OF A FEMALE AFRICAN ELEPHANT (TUSKS REMOVED)

Flat forehead

Eye

Pinna (ear flap)

Annulus (ring) of trunk

Belly

Foreleg

Trunk (proboscis)

Upper "lip" of trunk

Lower "lip" of trunk

SKULL OF AN ASIAN ELEPHANT

Orbit

Cranium

Maxilla

Premaxilla

Jugal bar

Tusk (upper incisor)

Upper molars

Lower molars

Mandible

SKELETON OF AN AFRICAN ELEPHANT (TUSKS REMOVED)

Cervical vertebrae

Thoracolumbar vertebrae

Skull

Sacrum

Mandible

Caudal vertebrae

Scapula

Sternum

Pelvis

Rib

Femur

Humerus

Radius

Ulna

Patella

Tibia

Carpals

Metacarpals

Fibula

Phalanx

Tarsals

Phalanx

Metatarsals

Primates

THE MAMMALIAN ORDER PRIMATES consists of monkeys, apes, and their relatives (including humans). There are two suborders of primates: Prosimii, the primitive primates, which include lemurs, tarsiers, and lorises; and Anthropoidea, the advanced primates, which include monkeys, apes, and humans. The anthropoids are divided into New World monkeys, Old World monkeys, and hominids. New World monkeys typically have wide-apart nostrils that open to the side; and long tails, which are prehensile (grasping) in some species. This group of monkeys lives in South America, and includes marmosets, tamarins, and howler monkeys. Old World monkeys typically have close-set nostrils that open forwards or downwards; and non-prehensile tails. This group of monkeys lives in Africa and Asia, and includes langurs, mandrills, macaques, and baboons. Hominids typically have large brains, and no tail. This group includes the apes—chimpanzees, gibbons, gorillas, and orangutans—and humans.

INTERNAL ANATOMY OF A FEMALE CHIMPANZEE

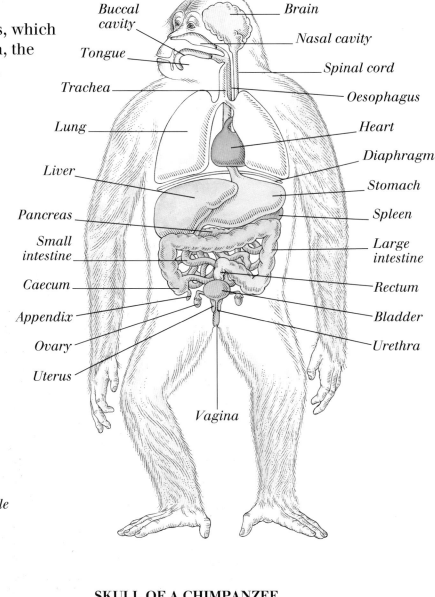

Buccal cavity
Brain
Tongue
Nasal cavity
Trachea
Spinal cord
Oesophagus
Lung
Heart
Liver
Diaphragm
Stomach
Pancreas
Spleen
Small intestine
Large intestine
Caecum
Rectum
Appendix
Bladder
Ovary
Urethra
Uterus
Vagina

SKELETON OF A RHESUS MONKEY

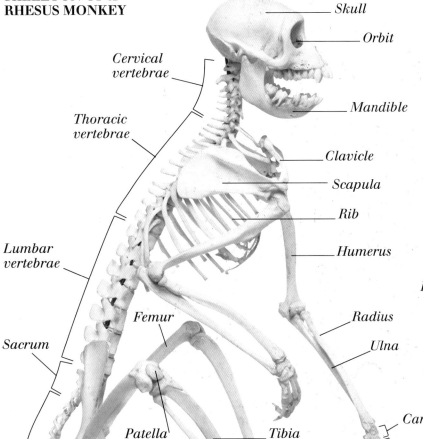

Skull
Orbit
Cervical vertebrae
Thoracic vertebrae
Mandible
Clavicle
Scapula
Rib
Lumbar vertebrae
Humerus
Femur
Radius
Sacrum
Ulna
Patella
Tibia
Carpals
Metacarpals
Fibula
Pelvis
Phalanges
Caudal vertebrae
Tarsals
Metatarsals
Phalanges

SKULL OF A CHIMPANZEE

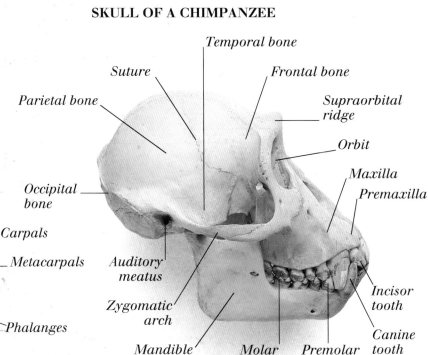

Temporal bone
Suture
Frontal bone
Parietal bone
Supraorbital ridge
Orbit
Occipital bone
Maxilla
Premaxilla
Auditory meatus
Zygomatic arch
Incisor tooth
Mandible
Molar tooth
Premolar tooth
Canine tooth

EXAMPLES OF PRIMATES

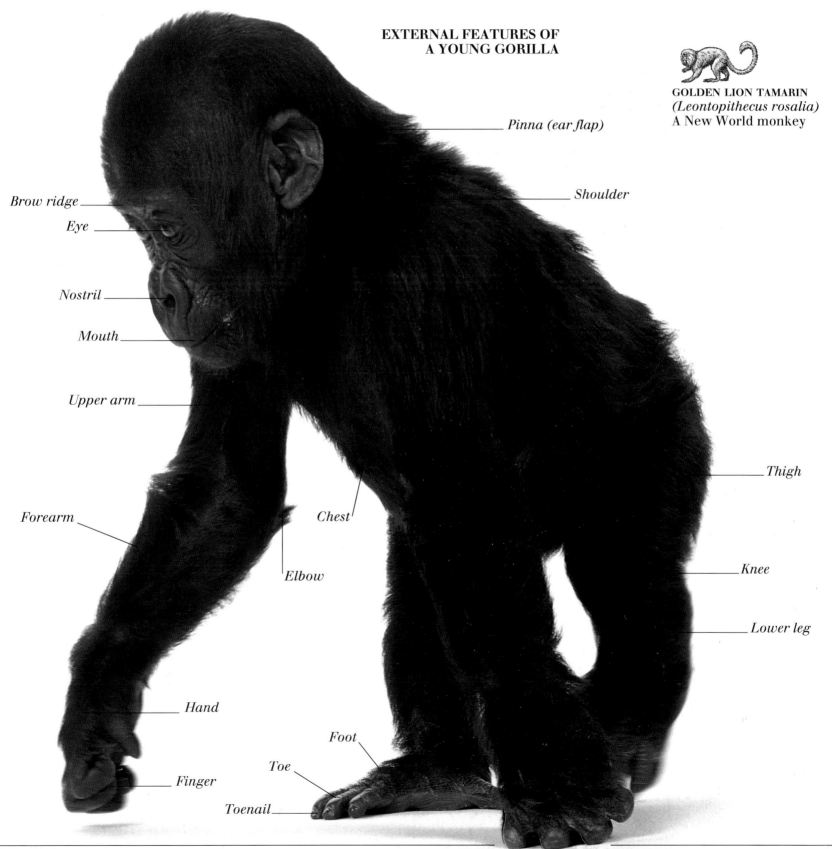

RING-TAILED LEMUR
(Lemur catta)
A prosimian

MALE RED HOWLER MONKEY
(Alouatta seniculus)
A New World monkey

MALE MANDRILL
(Mandrillus sphinx)
An Old World monkey

CHIMPANZEE
(Pan troglodytes)
An ape

EXTERNAL FEATURES OF
A YOUNG GORILLA

GOLDEN LION TAMARIN
(Leontopithecus rosalia)
A New World monkey

Pinna (ear flap)

Brow ridge

Eye

Shoulder

Nostril

Mouth

Upper arm

Thigh

Forearm

Chest

Elbow

Knee

Lower leg

Hand

Foot

Finger

Toe

Toenail

Dolphins, whales, and seals

DOLPHINS, WHALES, AND SEALS belong to
two orders of mammals adapted to living
in water. Dolphins and whales make up the
order Cetacea. Typical cetacean features include
a streamlined, fish-like shape; forelimbs in the form
of flippers; no visible hind limbs; a horizontally flattened
tail; and thick blubber under the skin. There are two groups
of cetaceans: toothed whales, including sperm whales, white whales,
beaked whales, dolphins, and porpoises; and the larger whalebone (baleen)
whales, including rorquals, grey whales, and right whales. The blue whale—a
rorqual—is the largest living animal: an adult may be up to 30 m (100 ft) long
and weigh 130 tonnes (128 tons). Seals and their relatives—sea lions and
walruses—make up the order Pinnipedia. Characteristically, they have a
streamlined, torpedo-shaped body; forelimbs and hind limbs modified as
flippers; thick blubber; and no external ears.

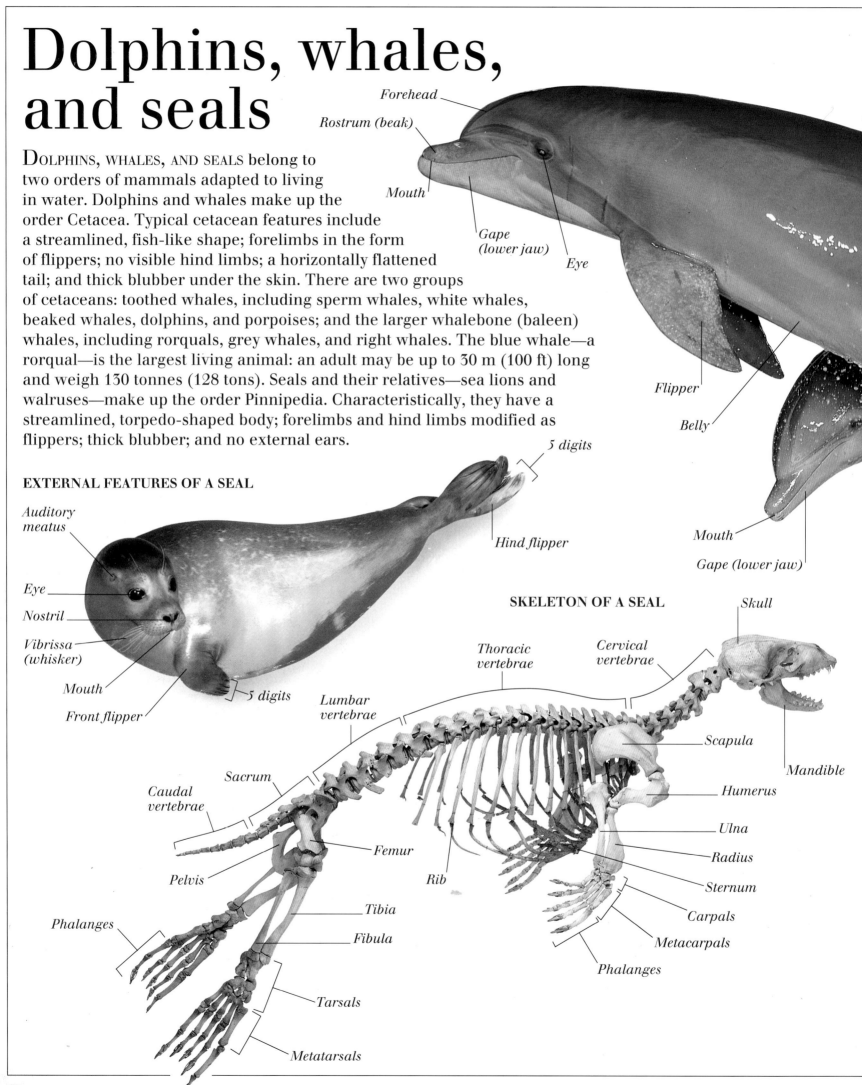

Forehead

Rostrum (beak)

Mouth

Gape
(lower jaw)

Eye

Flipper

Belly

Mouth

Gape (lower jaw)

EXTERNAL FEATURES OF A SEAL

Auditory
meatus

5 digits

Hind flipper

Eye

Nostril

Vibrissa
(whisker)

Mouth

Front flipper

5 digits

SKELETON OF A SEAL

Thoracic
vertebrae

Cervical
vertebrae

Skull

Lumbar
vertebrae

Scapula

Mandible

Sacrum

Humerus

Caudal
vertebrae

Femur

Ulna

Pelvis

Rib

Radius

Sternum

Tibia

Carpals

Phalanges

Fibula

Metacarpals

Phalanges

Tarsals

Metatarsals

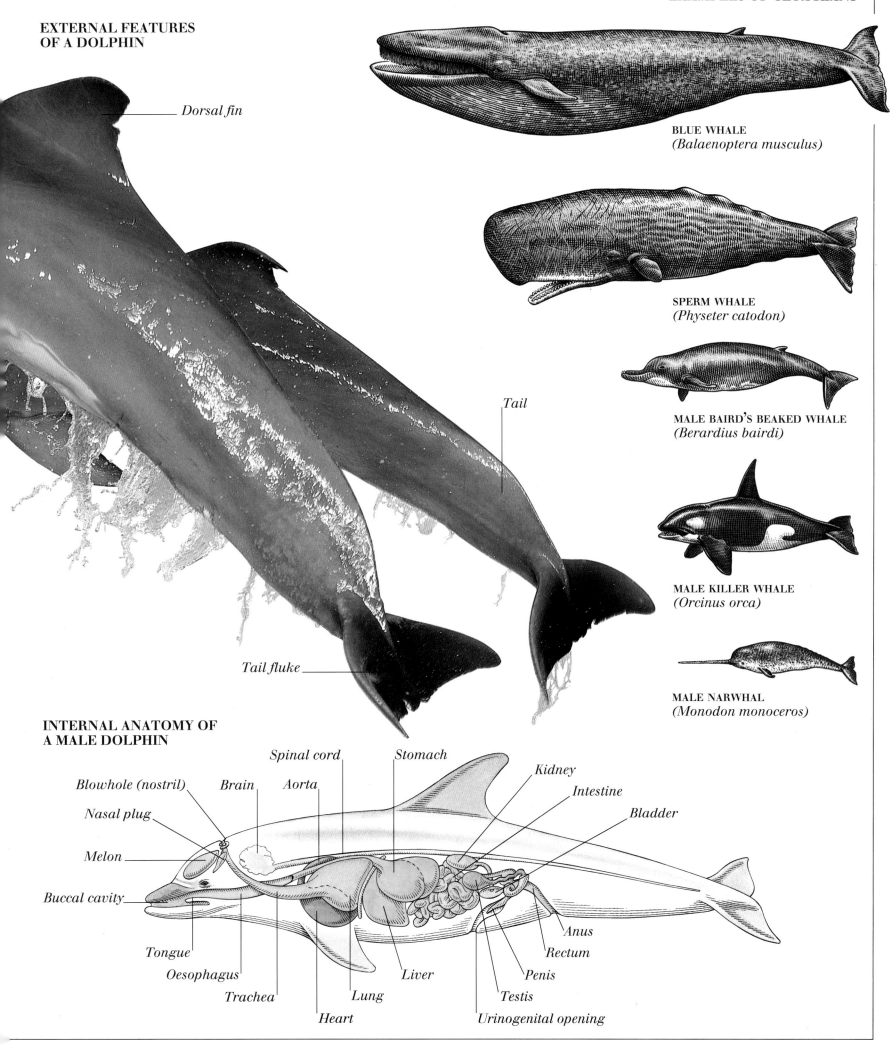

**EXTERNAL FEATURES
OF A DOLPHIN**

Dorsal fin

Tail

Tail fluke

BLUE WHALE
(*Balaenoptera musculus*)

SPERM WHALE
(*Physeter catodon*)

MALE BAIRD'S BEAKED WHALE
(*Berardius bairdi*)

MALE KILLER WHALE
(*Orcinus orca*)

MALE NARWHAL
(*Monodon monoceros*)

**INTERNAL ANATOMY OF
A MALE DOLPHIN**

Spinal cord

Stomach

Kidney

Intestine

Blowhole (nostril)

Brain

Aorta

Bladder

Nasal plug

Melon

Buccal cavity

Anus

Rectum

Tongue

Penis

Oesophagus

Testis

Trachea

Liver

Heart

Lung

Urinogenital opening

Marsupials and Monotremes

MARSUPIALS AND MONOTREMES are two orders of mammals that differ from other mammalian groups in the ways that their young develop. The order Marsupalia, the pouched mammals, is made up of kangaroos and their relatives. Typically, marsupials give birth to their young at a very early stage of development. The young then crawls to the mother's pouch (which is on the outside of her abdomen), where it attaches itself to a nipple and remains until fully developed. Most marsupials live in Australia, although the opossums—which are classified as marsupials despite not having a pouch—live in the Americas. The order Monotremata is made up of the platypus and its relatives (the echidnas, or spiny anteaters). The monotremes are primitive mammals that lay eggs, which the mother incubates. The monotremes are found only in Australia and New Guinea.

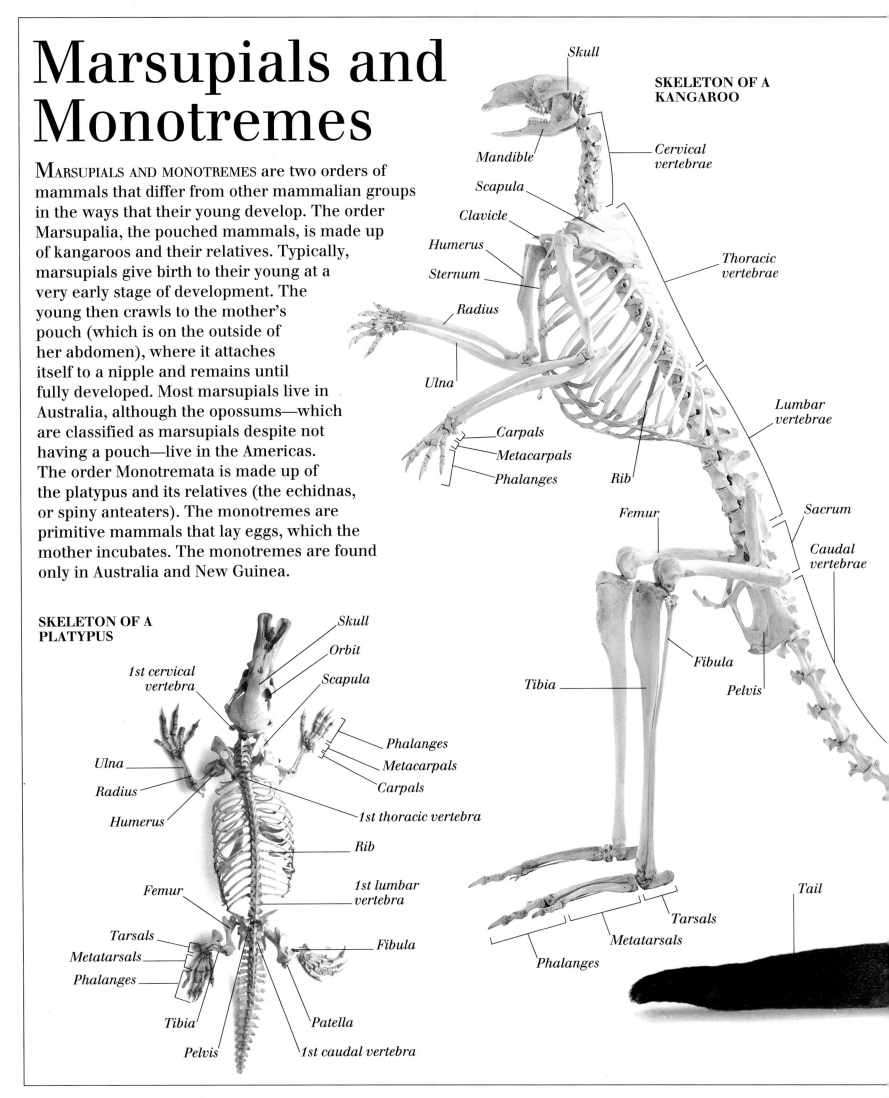

SKELETON OF A KANGAROO

Skull
Mandible
Cervical vertebrae
Scapula
Clavicle
Humerus
Sternum
Radius
Ulna
Thoracic vertebrae
Lumbar vertebrae
Carpals
Metacarpals
Phalanges
Rib
Femur
Sacrum
Caudal vertebrae
Fibula
Tibia
Pelvis
Tail
Tarsals
Metatarsals
Phalanges

SKELETON OF A PLATYPUS

Skull
Orbit
1st cervical vertebra
Scapula
Ulna
Radius
Phalanges
Metacarpals
Carpals
Humerus
1st thoracic vertebra
Rib
Femur
1st lumbar vertebra
Tarsals
Metatarsals
Phalanges
Fibula
Tibia
Patella
Pelvis
1st caudal vertebra

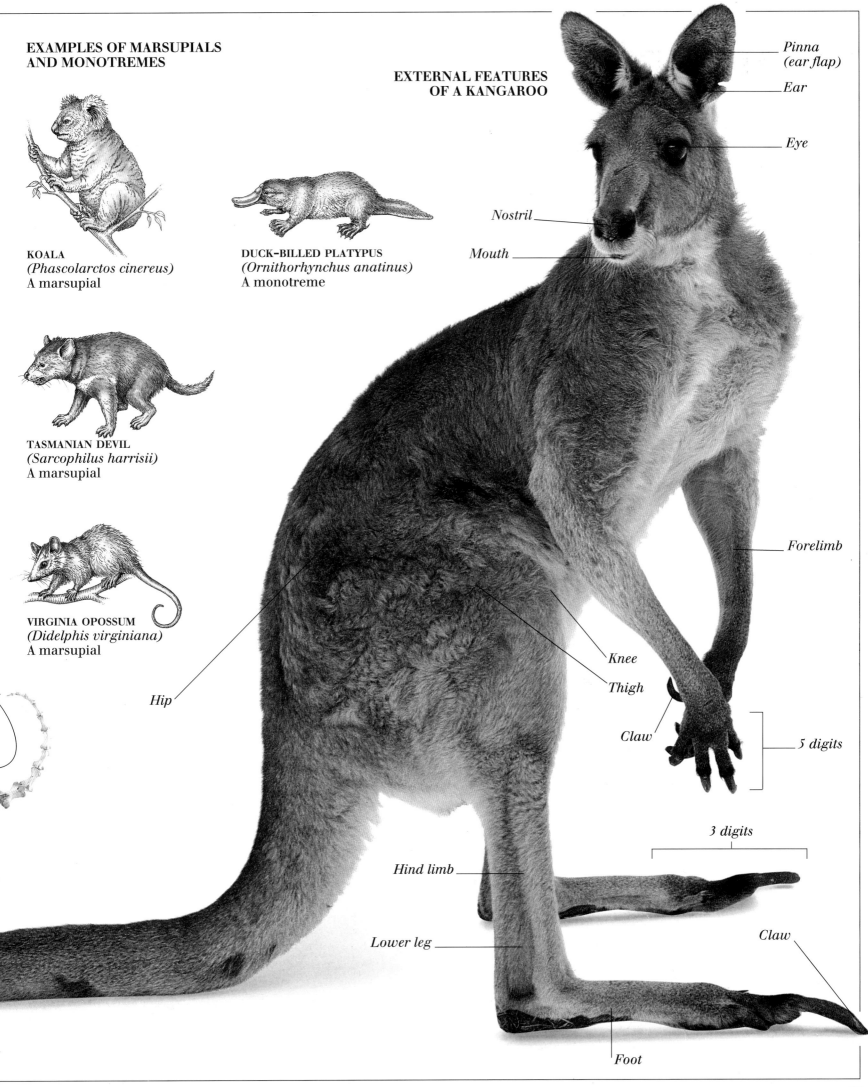

**EXAMPLES OF MARSUPIALS
AND MONOTREMES**

KOALA
(Phascolarctos cinereus)
A marsupial

DUCK-BILLED PLATYPUS
(Ornithorhynchus anatinus)
A monotreme

TASMANIAN DEVIL
(Sarcophilus harrisii)
A marsupial

VIRGINIA OPOSSUM
(Didelphis virginiana)
A marsupial

**EXTERNAL FEATURES
OF A KANGAROO**

*Pinna
(ear flap)*

Ear

Eye

Nostril

Mouth

Forelimb

Hip

Knee

Thigh

Claw

5 digits

3 digits

Hind limb

Lower leg

Claw

Foot

55

Animal tracks

ANIMAL TRACKS ARE TEMPORARY RECORDS of the passage of land animals across impressionable surfaces, such as damp sand, mud, or snow. By examining tracks for the shape, size, and number of toes, claws, nails, hooves, or pads, it is often possible to identify the animal that made them. For example, the paw marks of mammals that walk on their toes, such as dogs and cats, can be differentiated by the shape and size of their pads. As well as identifying an animal, tracks can often reveal its way of life. For instance, the tracks made by web-footed ducks show that they are swimming birds, whereas the open-toed tracks of crows show that they are perching birds. In addition, the depth and pattern of tracks reveal whether the animal was walking, running, or hopping.

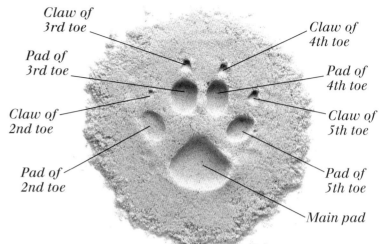

Claw of 3rd toe
Pad of 3rd toe
Claw of 2nd toe
Pad of 2nd toe
Claw of 4th toe
Pad of 4th toe
Claw of 5th toe
Pad of 5th toe
Main pad

RIGHT FOREFOOT OF A DOMESTIC DOG

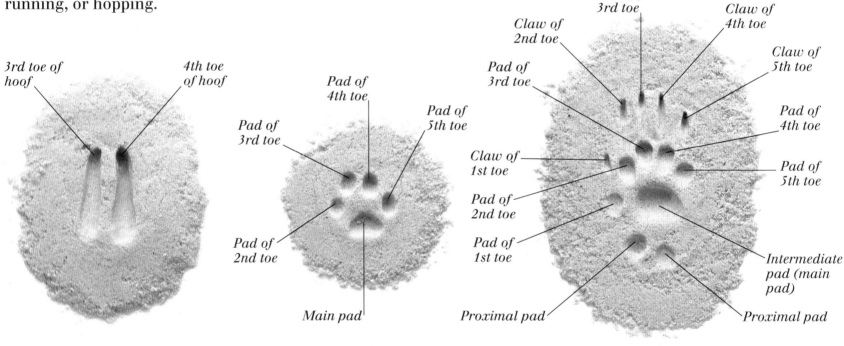

3rd toe of hoof
4th toe of hoof

RIGHT FOREFOOT OF A DOMESTIC SHEEP

Pad of 4th toe
Pad of 3rd toe
Pad of 5th toe
Pad of 2nd toe
Main pad

RIGHT FOREFOOT OF A DOMESTIC CAT

Claw of 3rd toe
Claw of 2nd toe
Pad of 3rd toe
Claw of 1st toe
Pad of 2nd toe
Pad of 1st toe
Proximal pad
Claw of 4th toe
Claw of 5th toe
Pad of 4th toe
Pad of 5th toe
Intermediate pad (main pad)
Proximal pad

RIGHT FOREFOOT OF A BADGER

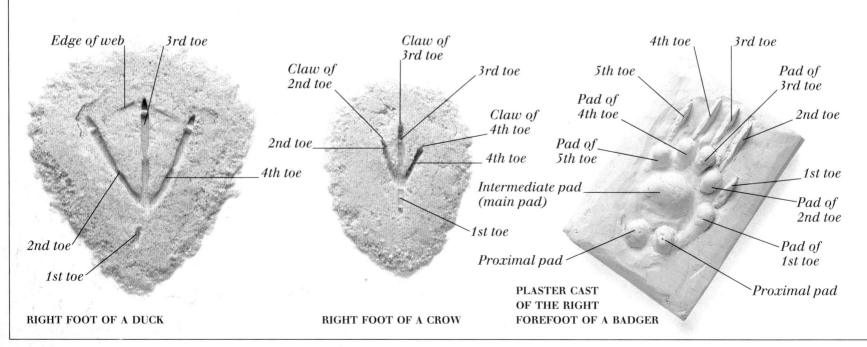

Edge of web
3rd toe
2nd toe
4th toe
1st toe

RIGHT FOOT OF A DUCK

Claw of 2nd toe
Claw of 3rd toe
3rd toe
Claw of 4th toe
2nd toe
4th toe
1st toe

RIGHT FOOT OF A CROW

4th toe
3rd toe
5th toe
Pad of 3rd toe
Pad of 4th toe
2nd toe
Pad of 5th toe
1st toe
Intermediate pad (main pad)
Pad of 2nd toe
Proximal pad
Pad of 1st toe
Proximal pad

PLASTER CAST OF THE RIGHT FOREFOOT OF A BADGER

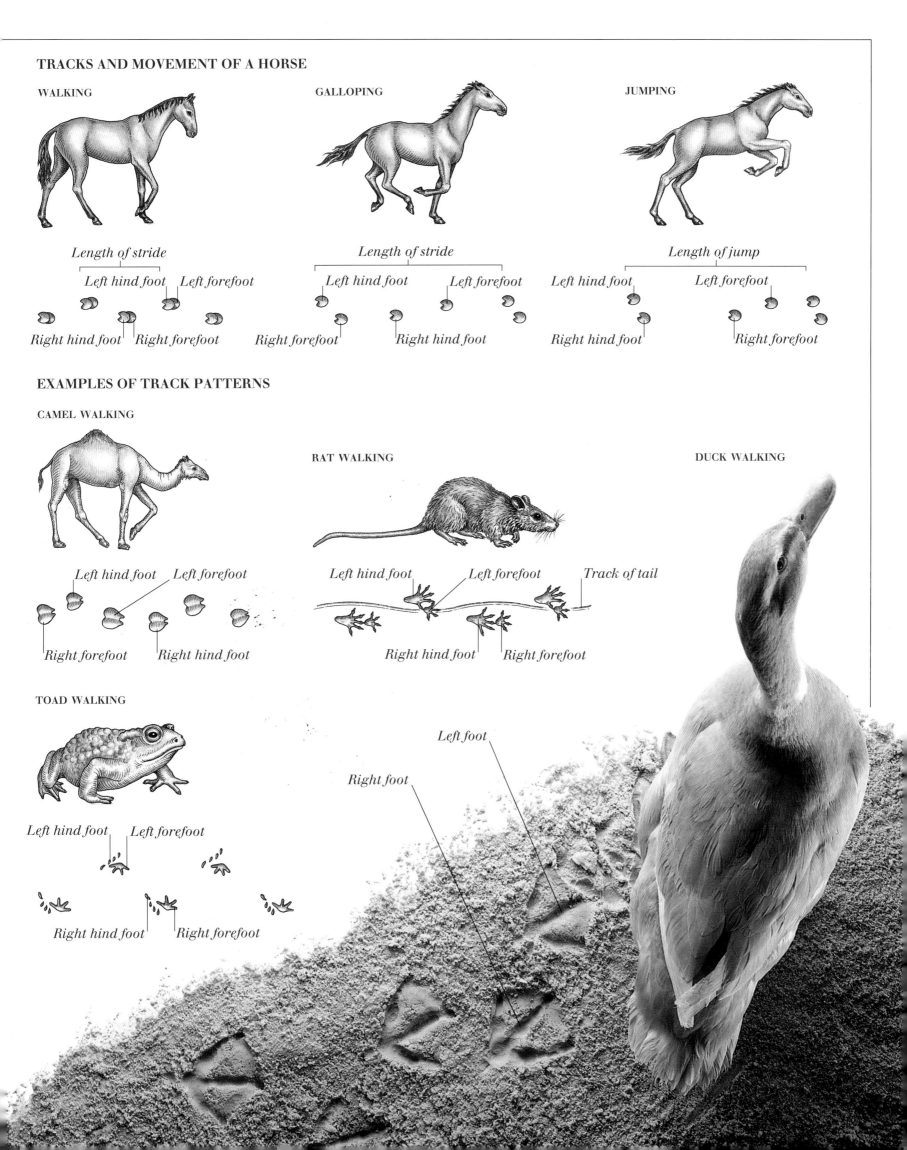

TRACKS AND MOVEMENT OF A HORSE

WALKING

Length of stride

Left hind foot *Left forefoot*

Right hind foot *Right forefoot*

GALLOPING

Length of stride

Left hind foot *Left forefoot*

Right forefoot *Right hind foot*

JUMPING

Length of jump

Left hind foot *Left forefoot*

Right hind foot *Right forefoot*

EXAMPLES OF TRACK PATTERNS

CAMEL WALKING

Left hind foot *Left forefoot*

Right forefoot *Right hind foot*

RAT WALKING

Left hind foot *Left forefoot* *Track of tail*

Right hind foot *Right forefoot*

TOAD WALKING

Left hind foot *Left forefoot*

Right hind foot *Right forefoot*

DUCK WALKING

Left foot

Right foot

Animal classification

Biologists use a universal system to classify animals and other organisms. All animals form one large grouping, the kingdom Animalia. The kingdom is subdivided into progressively smaller groups on the basis of similarities among animals within each group, and their differences from animals in other groups. The result of this repeated subdivision is a "family tree" of the animal world. First, the kingdom Animalia is divided into several phyla (singular: phylum)—for example, phylum Chordata, which includes all animals with backbones, such as birds, fish, and mammals. Each phylum is divided into classes, and each class into orders. Every order contains a number of families, each of which is split into genera (singular: genus). Finally, each genus is divided into species. In some cases, additional levels of classification may be used. These extra levels are indicated by prefixes, such as "super-" and "sub-". In addition to the formal biological classification, animals are often divided into two main groups: vertebrates and invertebrates. Vertebrates have a backbone (vertebral column), whereas invertebrates do not. The chart shows the main groups in the animal kingdom.

KINGDOM ANIMALIA

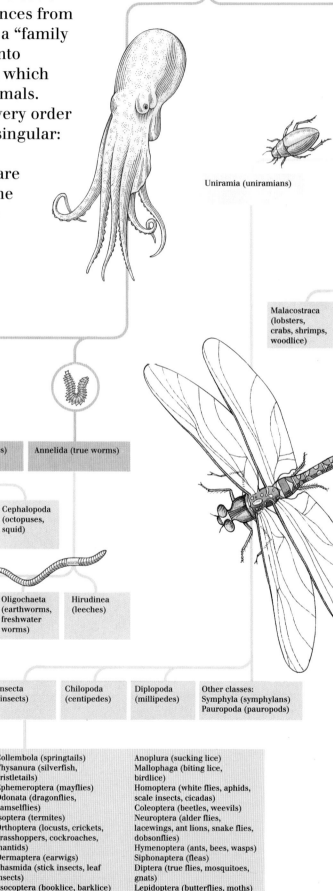

Uniramia (uniramians)

Malacostraca (lobsters, crabs, shrimps, woodlice)

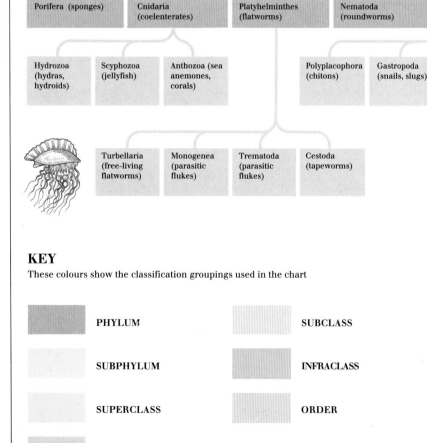

Porifera (sponges)

Cnidaria (coelenterates)

- Hydrozoa (hydras, hydroids)
- Scyphozoa (jellyfish)
- Anthozoa (sea anemones, corals)

Platyhelminthes (flatworms)

- Turbellaria (free-living flatworms)
- Monogenea (parasitic flukes)
- Trematoda (parasitic flukes)
- Cestoda (tapeworms)

Nematoda (roundworms)

Mollusca (molluscs)

- Polyplacophora (chitons)
- Gastropoda (snails, slugs)
- Bivalvia (clams, scallops, mussels)
- Cephalopoda (octopuses, squid)

Annelida (true worms)

- Polychaeta (marine worms)
- Oligochaeta (earthworms, freshwater worms)
- Hirudinea (leeches)

Insecta (insects)   Chilopoda (centipedes)   Diplopoda (millipedes)   Other classes: Symphyla (symphylans) Pauropoda (pauropods)

KEY

These colours show the classification groupings used in the chart

PHYLUM	SUBCLASS
SUBPHYLUM	INFRACLASS
SUPERCLASS	ORDER
CLASS	

Collembola (springtails)
Thysanura (silverfish, bristletails)
Ephemeroptera (mayflies)
Odonata (dragonflies, damselflies)
Isoptera (termites)
Orthoptera (locusts, crickets, grasshoppers, cockroaches, mantids)
Dermaptera (earwigs)
Phasmida (stick insects, leaf insects)
Psocoptera (booklice, barklice)
Hemiptera (true bugs)

Anoplura (sucking lice)
Mallophaga (biting lice, birdlice)
Homoptera (white flies, aphids, scale insects, cicadas)
Coleoptera (beetles, weevils)
Neuroptera (alder flies, lacewings, ant lions, snake flies, dobsonflies)
Hymenoptera (ants, bees, wasps)
Siphonaptera (fleas)
Diptera (true flies, mosquitoes, gnats)
Lepidoptera (butterflies, moths)

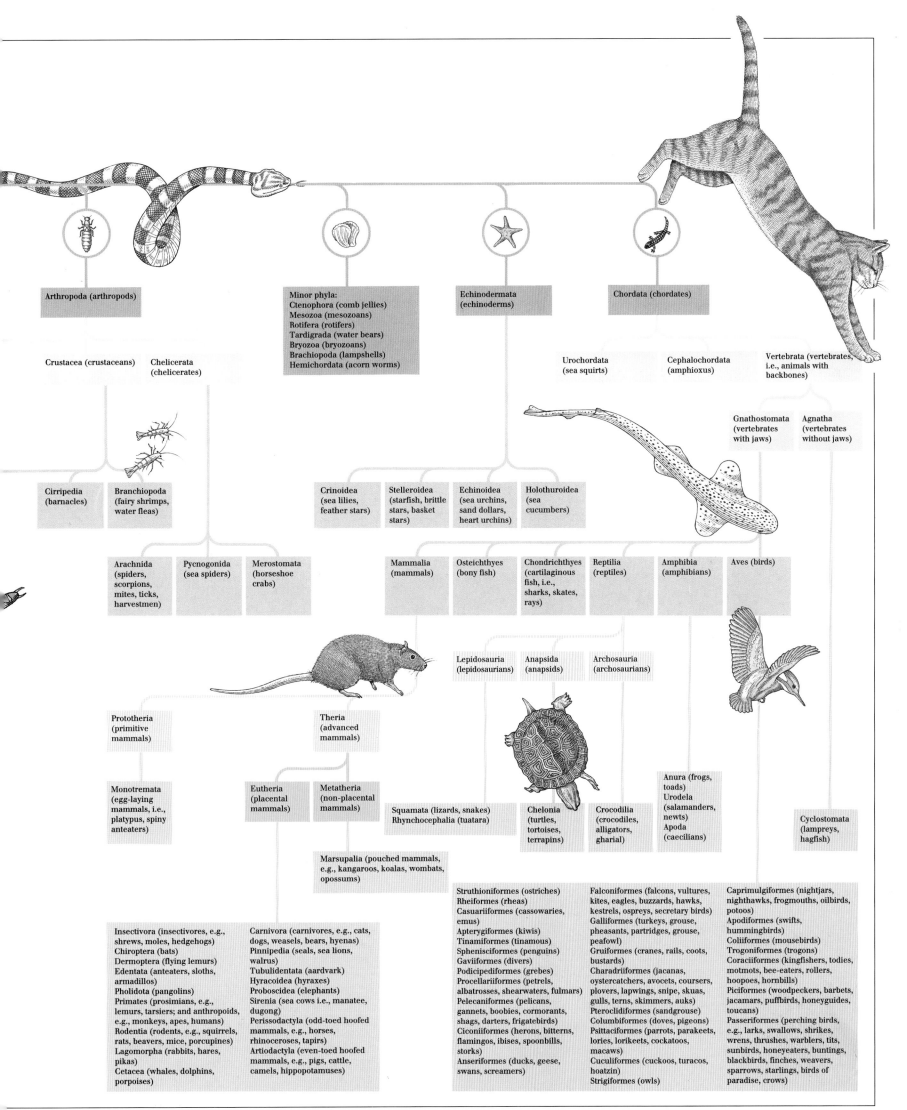

Arthropoda (arthropods)

Minor phyla:
Ctenophora (comb jellies)
Mesozoa (mesozoans)
Rotifera (rotifers)
Tardigrada (water bears)
Bryozoa (bryozoans)
Brachiopoda (lampshells)
Hemichordata (acorn worms)

Echinodermata (echinoderms)

Chordata (chordates)

Crustacea (crustaceans)

Chelicerata (chelicerates)

Urochordata (sea squirts)

Cephalochordata (amphioxus)

Vertebrata (vertebrates, i.e., animals with backbones)

Gnathostomata (vertebrates with jaws)

Agnatha (vertebrates without jaws)

Cirripedia (barnacles)

Branchiopoda (fairy shrimps, water fleas)

Crinoidea (sea lilies, feather stars)

Stelleroidea (starfish, brittle stars, basket stars)

Echinoidea (sea urchins, sand dollars, heart urchins)

Holothuroidea (sea cucumbers)

Arachnida (spiders, scorpions, mites, ticks, harvestmen)

Pycnogonida (sea spiders)

Merostomata (horseshoe crabs)

Mammalia (mammals)

Osteichthyes (bony fish)

Chondrichthyes (cartilaginous fish, i.e., sharks, skates, rays)

Reptilia (reptiles)

Amphibia (amphibians)

Aves (birds)

Lepidosauria (lepidosaurians)

Anapsida (anapsids)

Archosauria (archosaurians)

Prototheria (primitive mammals)

Theria (advanced mammals)

Anura (frogs, toads)
Urodela (salamanders, newts)
Apoda (caecilians)

Monotremata (egg-laying mammals, i.e., platypus, spiny anteaters)

Eutheria (placental mammals)

Metatheria (non-placental mammals)

Squamata (lizards, snakes)
Rhynchocephalia (tuatara)

Chelonia (turtles, tortoises, terrapins)

Crocodilia (crocodiles, alligators, gharial)

Cyclostomata (lampreys, hagfish)

Marsupalia (pouched mammals, e.g., kangaroos, koalas, wombats, opossums)

Insectivora (insectivores, e.g., shrews, moles, hedgehogs)
Chiroptera (bats)
Dermoptera (flying lemurs)
Edentata (anteaters, sloths, armadillos)
Pholidota (pangolins)
Primates (prosimians, e.g., lemurs, tarsiers; and anthropoids, e.g., monkeys, apes, humans)
Rodentia (rodents, e.g., squirrels, rats, beavers, mice, porcupines)
Lagomorpha (rabbits, hares, pikas)
Cetacea (whales, dolphins, porpoises)

Carnivora (carnivores, e.g., cats, dogs, weasels, bears, hyenas)
Pinnipedia (seals, sea lions, walrus)
Tubulidentata (aardvark)
Hyracoidea (hyraxes)
Proboscidea (elephants)
Sirenia (sea cows i.e., manatee, dugong)
Perissodactyla (odd-toed hoofed mammals, e.g., horses, rhinoceroses, tapirs)
Artiodactyla (even-toed hoofed mammals, e.g., pigs, cattle, camels, hippopotamuses)

Struthioniformes (ostriches)
Rheiformes (rheas)
Casuariiformes (cassowaries, emus)
Apterygiformes (kiwis)
Tinamiformes (tinamous)
Sphenisciformes (penguins)
Gaviiformes (divers)
Podicipediformes (grebes)
Procellariiformes (petrels, albatrosses, shearwaters, fulmars)
Pelecaniformes (pelicans, gannets, boobies, cormorants, shags, darters, frigatebirds)
Ciconiiformes (herons, bitterns, flamingos, ibises, spoonbills, storks)
Anseriformes (ducks, geese, swans, screamers)

Falconiformes (falcons, vultures, kites, eagles, buzzards, hawks, kestrels, ospreys, secretary birds)
Galliformes (turkeys, grouse, pheasants, partridges, grouse, peafowl)
Gruiformes (cranes, rails, coots, bustards)
Charadriiformes (jacanas, oystercatchers, avocets, coursers, plovers, lapwings, snipe, skuas, gulls, terns, skimmers, auks)
Pteroclidiformes (sandgrouse)
Columbiformes (doves, pigeons)
Psittaciformes (parrots, parakeets, lories, lorikeets, cockatoos, macaws)
Cuculiformes (cuckoos, turacos, hoatzin)
Strigiformes (owls)

Caprimulgiformes (nightjars, nighthawks, frogmouths, oilbirds, potoos)
Apodiformes (swifts, hummingbirds)
Coliiformes (mousebirds)
Trogoniformes (trogons)
Coraciiformes (kingfishers, todies, motmots, bee-eaters, rollers, hoopoes, hornbills)
Piciformes (woodpeckers, barbets, jacamars, puffbirds, honeyguides, toucans)
Passeriformes (perching birds, e.g., larks, swallows, shrikes, wrens, thrushes, warblers, tits, sunbirds, honeyeaters, buntings, blackbirds, finches, weavers, sparrows, starlings, birds of paradise, crows)

Index

A

Aardvarks 59
Abalones 26
Abdomen
  Ant 13
  Bee 12
  Beetle 13
  Butterfly 10-11
  Caterpillar 11
  Crab 28
  Crayfish 28
  Moth 10
  Rattlesnake 33
  Scorpion 14
  Shrimp 28
  Spider 15
Abdominal artery 29
Abdominal segment
  Butterfly 11
  Crayfish 28
Abomasum 46
Aboral surface
  Sea urchin 23
  Starfish 22
Acetabulum
  Blood fluke 17
  Leech 16
  Liver fluke 17
  Pork tapeworm 16
Acipenser sturio 20
Acorn worms 59
Actinia equina 24
Actinothoe sphyrodeta 24
Adder 8
Adductor muscle 29
Advanced mammals 59
African elephants 48-49
  Head 9
Agnatha 18, 59
Air sac 40
Albatrosses 59
Albumen 40
Albumen gland 27
Alder flies 58
Allantoic fluid 40
Allantois 40-41
Alligator mississippiensis 34
Alligators 34, 59
Alouatta seniculus 51
Alsatian dog 43
Alula 39
Ambulacral groove 23
American alligator 34
American beaver 45
American black bear 43
Amnion 40-41
Amniotic fluid 40
Amoebocyte 24
Amphibia 30, 59
Amphibians 6, 30-31, 59
Amphioxus 59
Ampulla
  Sea urchin 23
  Starfish 22
Anal clasper 11
Anal fin
  Bony fish 6, 20-21
  Lamprey 18
  Mackerel 6
Anal fin ray 20
Anal flap 48
Anapsida 59
Anapsids 59
Anemonia viridis 24
Anglerfish 20
Angular process 42
Animal bodies 6-7
Animal classification 58-59
Animal heads 8-9
Animalia 58
Animal tracks 56-57
Annelida 16, 58
Annulus of trunk 49
  Elephant 9
Anoplura 58
Anseriformes 59
Antelopes 46, 59
Antenna
  Ant 13
  Beetle 6, 9
  Bumblebee 12

Butterfly 10
  Caterpillar 11
  Crab 28
  Crayfish 29
  Insect 8
  Malacostraca 28
  Moth 10
  Shrimp 28
Antennule 29
Anterior aorta 14
Anterior chamber of cloaca 33
Anterior dorsal fin
  Bony fish 6, 21
  Dogfish 19
  Lamprey 18
  Mackerel 6
Anterior sucker 17
Anterior tentacle 27
Anterior testis 17
Anterior wing of shell 26
Anthozoa 24, 58
Anthropoidea 50
Anthropoids 50, 59
Ant lions 58
Ants 12-13, 58
Anura 30, 59
Anus
  Barnacle 29
  Bony fish 21
  Butterfly 10
  Cow 46
  Crayfish 29
  Dolphin 53
  Domestic cat 43
  Elephant 48
  Octopus 26
  Rabbit 44
  Sea urchin 23
  Snail 27
  Spider 14
  Starfish 22
  Tortoise 35
Aorta
  Anterior 14
  Bony fish 21
  Dogfish 19
  Dolphin 53
  Dorsal 13, 19, 21, 30
  Honeybee 13
  Posterior 14
  Spider 14
  Ventral 19
Apes 50-51, 59
Apex
  Beetle elytron 13
  Butterfly wing 11
  Snail shell 27
Aphids 58
Apoda 59
Apodiformes 59
Appendix
  Chimpanzee 50
  Rabbit 44
Apterygiformes 59
Aquiferous system 24
Ara ararauna 38
Arachnida 14, 59
Arachnids 14-15
Araneae 14
Archosauria 59
Archosaurians 59
Arm
  Gorilla 51
  Lion 42
  Starfish 7, 22
Armadillos 59
Artery
  Abdominal 29
  Epibranchial 19
  Orbital 19
  Pulmonary 30
  Sternal 29
Arthropoda 10, 12, 14, 28, 59
Arthropods 59
Artiodactyla 46-47, 59
Asian elephants 48-49
Asses 46
Asterias rubens 7, 23
Asterina gibbosa 23
Astragalus 31
Atlantic mackerel 6
Atlas 47

Atlas beetle 12
Atrium 24
Auditory meatus
  Chimpanzee 50
  Seal 52
Auks 59
Aves 36, 59
Axial gland 23
Axis 47
Aythya fuligula 36

B

Baboons 50
Back
  Elephant 48
  Horse 46
  Lion 43
Bactrian camel 47
Badgers 42
  Tracks 56
Baird's beaked whale 53
Balaenoptera musculus 53
Balanophyllia regia 25
Baleen whales 52
Baltimore oriole 41
Banded milk snake 7, 32
Barb 25
Barbets 59
Barklice 58
Barnacle 29
Barnacles 28-29, 59
Basal disc 25
Basis 29
Basket stars 22, 59
Basking shark 19
Bats 59
Beadlet anemone 24
Beak
  Birds 36-38
  Chelonian 34
  Dolphin 53
  Hatching chick 40-41
  Kestrel 6
  Lory 8
  Octopus 26
Beaked whales 52
Bears 42-43, 59
Beavers 44-45, 59
Bee-eaters 59
Bee hummingbird 41
Bees 12-13, 58
Beetles 12-13, 58
  Exoskeleton 6
  Goliath 8
  Legs 6
  Longhorn 6
Belly
  Bird 36
  Caiman 34
  Dolphin 52
  Elephant 49
  Horse 46
  Lion 43
  Lizard 32
Berardius bairdi 53
Bile duct 37
Birdlice 58
Bird of paradise 59
Bird of prey 7, 36
Birds 36-39, 59
  Beaks 7-8, 38
  Feathers 7, 39
  Feet 38
  Wing 39
Biting lice 58
Bitis arietans 8
Bitterns 59
Bivalvia 26, 58
Blackbacked gull 41
Blackbirds 59
Blackheaded gull 37
Black rhinoceros 47
Black widow spider 15
Bladder
  Bony fish 21
  Chimpanzee 50
  Dolphin 53
  Domestic cat 43
  Elephant 48
  Excretory 17
  Lizard 33
  Rabbit 44

Swim bladder 18, 20-21
  Tortoise 35
  Urinary 21
Blood flukes 16-17
Blood vessel
  Butterfly 10
  Earthworm 16
Blowhole 53
Blubber 52
Blue-and-yellow macaw 38
Blue-spotted sea bream 8
Blue-streaked lory 8
Blue whales 52-53
Bodies 6-7
Body cavity 16
Body sections
  Ant 12
  Bee 12
  Beetle 12
  Butterfly 10
  Moth 10
  Scorpion 14
  Spider 14-15
Bony fish 20-21, 59
  Body 6
  Heads 8
Boobies 59
Booklice 58
Book lung 14
Brachiopoda 59
Brain 8
  Bird 37
  Bony fish 21
  Butterfly 10
  Chimpanzee 50
  Crayfish 29
  Dogfish 19
  Domestic cat 43
  Dolphin 53
  Elephant 48
  Hominid 50
  Honeybee 13
  Lizard 33
  Octopus 26
  Rabbit 44
  Spider 14
Branchial heart 26
Branchiopoda 59
Branchiostegal ray 21
Breast
  Bird 36
  Horse 47
Breathing 8
  Fish 20
Bristletails 58
Brittle stars 22-23, 59
Bronchus 30
Brow ridge 51
Bryozoa 59
Bryozoans 59
Buccal cavity
  Bird 37
  Chimpanzee 50
  Dolphin 53
  Domestic cat 43
  Elephant 48
  Rabbit 44
  Tortoise 35
Buccal mass 26
Bumblebees 12-13
Buntings 59
Bustards 59
Butterflies 10-11, 58
Buttock 46
Buzzards 59

C

Caecilians 59
Caecum
  Bird 37
  Chimpanzee 50
  Cow 46
  Digestive 26, 29
  Gut 14
  Intestinal 17
  Octopus 26
  Pyloric 21-22
  Rabbit 44
  Rectal 22
Caimans 34-35

Calamus 39
Calcaneum
  Frog 31
  Horse 47
Calcareous plates 28
Calcite ossicles 22
Californian purple sea urchin 23
Calipogen barbatus 6
Calliactis parasitica 24
Calypte helenae 41
Camels 46-47, 59
  Tracks 57
Camelus ferus 47
Camouflage coloration
  Quail's egg 40
  Tiger 7
Canal
  Sea urchin 23
  Starfish 22
Canine teeth
  Bear 42
  Chimpanzee 50
  Lion 42
Canis familiaris 43
Cannon bone 46-47
Capybara 44-45
Carapace 28-29
  Terrapin 35
Cardiac region of stomach 19
Cardiac stomach 22
Carina plate 29
Carnassial teeth 42
Carnivora 42, 59
Carnivores 42-43, 59
Carp 20
Carpals
  Bird 37
  Bird's wing 39
  Domestic cat 43
  Elephant 48
  Frog 31
  Hare 45
  Horse 47
  Kangaroo 54
  Lizard 32
  Platypus 54
  Rhesus monkey 50
  Seal 52
Carpus
  Crab 28
  Crayfish 29
Carrion crow 41
Cartilage 20
Cartilaginous fish 18-19, 20, 59
Cassowaries 36, 59
Castor canadensis 45
Casuariformes 59
Caterpillars 11
  Eggs 40
Cats 42-43, 59
  Tracks 56
Cattle 46, 59
Caudal fin
  Bony fish 6, 20-21
  Dogfish 19
  Lamprey 18
  Mackerel 6
Caudal fin ray 20
Caudal vertebrae
  Crocodile 34
  Domestic cat 43
  Elephant 49
  Hare 45
  Horse 47
  Kangaroo 54
  Lizard 32-33
  Platypus 54
  Rhesus monkey 50
  Seal 52
Caulophryne jordani 20
Cavies 44
Cell
  Collar 24
  Epidermal 24
  Pore 24
Cement gland 29
Centipedes 59
Central disc 7
Central shield 35
Centrum 35

Calamus 39
Cephalic groove 29
Cephalic vein 26
Cephalochordata 59
Cephalopoda 26, 58
Cephalopod mollusc 7
Cephalothorax
  Crayfish 29
  Malacostraca 28
  Scorpion 14
  Shrimp 28
  Spider 14-15
Cerebral ganglion
  Butterfly 9
  Earthworm 16
  Snail 27
Cervical vertebrae
  Bird 37
  Crocodile 34
  Domestic cat 43
  Elephant 49
  Hare 45
  Horse 47
  Kangaroo 54
  Lizard 32
  Platypus 54
  Rhesus monkey 50
  Seal 52
Cervus elephas 47
Cestoda 58
Cetacea 52, 59
Cetaceans 52-53
Cetorhinus maximus 19
Chafer beetle 12
Chaffinch 41
Chalcosoma atlas 12
Chambers of stomach 46
Charadriiformes 59
Cheek 47
Cheek pouches 44
Cheek teeth 42
Chela
  Crab 28
  Crayfish 29
  Scorpion 14
Chelicerae
  Scorpion 14
  Spider 14-15
Chelicerata 59
Chelicerates 59
Cheliped
  Crab 28
  Crayfish 29
Chelonia 34, 59
Chest
  Gorilla 51
  Lion 42
Chestnut 46
Chicken's egg 40
Chilopoda 58
Chimpanzees 50-51
Chin 36
Chin groove 47
Chipmunks 44
Chiroptera 59
Chitons 59
Choanocyte 24
Chondrichthyes 18, 59
Chordata 58-59
Chordates 59
Chorioallantoic membrane 40
Chrysalis 11
Chrysocyon brachyurus 43
Cicadas 58
Ciconia ciconia 36
Ciconiiformes 59
Circumoesophageal vessel 16
Cirri 28
Cirripedia 28, 59
Cirrus 29
Civets 42
Clams 26, 58
Classes 58
Classification 58-59
Clavicle
  Bird 37
  Bony fish 21
  Kangaroo 54
  Rhesus monkey 50
Claw
  Badger 56
  Beetle 13

Bird 36
Bumblebee 12
Caiman 35
Chick 41
Crab 28
Crayfish 29
Crow 56
Dog 56
Kangaroo 55
Lizard 32
Scorpion 14
Spider 15
Terrapin 35
Tracks 56
Clawed feet 38, 54
Clitellum 17
Cloaca
  Bird 37
  Dogfish 19
  Frog 30
  Lizard 33
  Spider 14
  Tortoise 35
Cloacal opening 33
Cloven hoof 46
Cnidaria 24, 58
Cnidocil 25
Cnidocytes 24-25
Cockatoos 59
Cockroaches 58
Cod 20
Coelenterata 24
Coelenterates 58
Coelom 16
Coleoptera 12, 58
Coliformes 59
Collar
  Sea anemone 25
  Snail 27
Collar cell 24
Collembola 58
Colon
  Butterfly 10
  Cow 46
  Rabbit 44
Columbiformes 59
Comb jellies 59
Common Atlantic mackerel 6
Common blackheaded gull 37
Common brittle star 23
Common kestrel 7
Common starfish 7, 23
Common tern 41
Complete mesentery 25
Compound eye
  Ant 13
  Bee 12
  Beetle 6, 8, 13
  Butterfly 10
  Crab 28
  Crayfish 29
  Malacostraca 28
  Shrimp 28
Condylactis sp. 24
Condyle 42
Constrictor snakes 32
Coots 59
Copulatory bursa
  Butterfly 10
  Snail 27
Coraciiformes 59
Coracoid
  Bird 37
  Turtle 35
Corals 24-25, 58
Cormorants 59
Coronet 46
Coronoid process 42
Corvus corone 41
Corynactis viridis 24
Costal margin
  Beetle 13
  Butterfly 11
Costal shield 35
Coursers 59
Courtship display 36
Coverts 36, 39
Cows 46
Coxa
  Beetle 13
  Crayfish 29
  Scorpion 14

Crabs 28, 58
Cranes 59
Cranium 49
Crayfish 28-29
Crest
　Horse 47
　Iguana 9
　Lizard 32
Crested porcupine 45
Crickets 58
Crinoidea 59
Crocodiles 54-35, 59
Crocodilia 34, 59
Crocodilians 54-35
Crocodylus niloticus 34
Crop
　Bird 37
　Butterfly 10
　Earthworm 16
　Honeybee 13
　Octopus 26
　Snail 27
Croup 46
Crown
　Bird 36
　Elephant 9
Crows 59
　Egg 41
　Tracks 56
Crustacea 28, 59
Crustaceans 14, 28-29, 59
Ctenidium 26
Ctenophora 59
Cuckoos 59
Cuculiformes 59
Cud 46
Cushion star 23
Cuttlefish 26
Cyclostomata 18, 59

D

Dactylus
　Crab 28
　Crayfish 29
Damselflies 58
Darters 59
Dart sac 27
Deer 46-47
Dentary 21
Dermaptera 58
Dermoptera 59
Dewlap
　Iguana 9
　Lizard 32
Diaphragm
　Chimpanzee 50
　Domestic cat 43
　Elephant 48
　Rabbit 44
Diceros bicornis 47
Didelphis virginiana 55
Digestive caecum
　Barnacle 29
　Crayfish 29
　Octopus 26
Digestive gland
　Snail 27
　Spider 14
Digestive system
　Cow 46
Digits
　Bird 37
　Bird's wing 39
　Frog 30
　Kangaroo 55
　Rabbit 44-45
　Rat 44
　Salamander 30
　Seal 52
Diplopoda 58
Diptera 58
Disc
　Basal 25
　Central 7
　Crab 24-25
　Pedal 25
　Sea anemone 24-25
　Starfish 7, 22
Distal tarsals 31
Divers 59
Dobsonflies 58
Dogfish 18-19
　Eggs 40
Dogs 42-43, 59
　Tracks 56
Dolomedes fimbriatus 15
Dolphins 52-53, 59
Domestic cat 43
　Tracks 56

Domestic dog 56
Dorsal abdominal artery 29
Dorsal aorta
　Bony fish 21
　Dogfish 19
　Frog 30
　Honeybee 13
Dorsal blood vessel
　Butterfly 10
　Earthworm 16
Dorsal fin
　Bony fish 6, 8, 21
　Dogfish 19
　Dolphin 53
　Lamprey 18
　Mackerel 6
　Sea bream 8
Dorsal fin ray 21
Dorsal mantle cavity 26
Dorsal margin of shell 26
Dorsal scale
　Caiman 34
　Lizard 32
Dorsal surface
　Earthworm 17
　Leech 16
Doves 59
Down 41
Downcurved edge 39
Dragonflies 58
Drone bumblebee 12
Duck-billed platypus 54-55, 59
Ducks 36, 59
　Tracks 56-57
Dugong 59
Duodenum
　Bird 37
　Cow 46
　Elephant 48
　Frog 30
　Rabbit 44
　Tortoise 35
Dynastes hercules 12

E

Eagles 59
Ear 8
　Elephants 9, 48
　Hare 44
　Horse 46
　Kangaroo 55
　Rabbit 9, 44
　Rat 44
Eardrum
　Chick 41
　Frog 30
　Iguana 9
　Lizard 32
Ear flap
　Elephant 9, 48-49
　Gorilla 51
　Kangaroo 55
　Rabbit 9, 44
　Rat 44
　Tiger 6
Earthworms 58
　External features 16
　Internal anatomy 16
Earwigs 58
Echidna nebulosa 20
Echidnas 54
Echinodermata 22, 59
Echinoderms 22, 59
　Body 7
Echinoidea 59
Echinus escelentus 23
Ectoderm 25
Edentata 59
Edible sea urchin 23
Eel 20
Egg-laying mammals 59
Eggs 40-41
　Baltimore oriole 41
　Bee hummingbird 41
　Bird 36
　Butterfly 11
　Capsule 40
　Carrion crow 41
　Case 40
　Chaffinch 41
　Chicken 41
　Common tern 41
　Dogfish 40
　Frog 30-31, 40
　Giant stick insect 40
　Greater backbacked gull 41

Hatching 40-41
Indian stick insect 40
Leaf insect 40
Liver fluke 17
Membranes 41
Moth 11
Ostrich 41
Quail 40-41
Reptile 32
Willow grouse 41
Egg-tooth 40-41
Egg white 40
Elasmobranchs 18
Elbow
　Gorilla 51
　Horse 47
　Lion 42
Elephants 48-49, 59
　Head 9
Elephas maximus 48
Elytra 12
Elytron 13
　Beetle 6
Emus 59
Endoderm 25
Endopod 28
Endoskeleton 22
Eos reticulata 8
Ephemeroptera 58
Epibranchial artery 19
Epidermal cell 24
Epiglottis 48
Euathlus emilia 14
Eutheria 59
Even-toed hoofed mammals 59
Even-toed ungulates 46-47
Excretory bladder 17
Excretory duct 17
Excretory pore 17, 27
Excurrent pore 24
Exoccipital bone 31
Exopod 28
Exoskeleton
　Ant 12
　Bee 12
　Beetle 6, 12
　Butterfly 10
　Malacstraca 28
　Moth 10
　Spider 15
External nostril 32
External skeleton
　Ant 12
　Bee 12
　Beetle 6, 12
　Butterfly 10
　Malacostraca 28
　Moth 10
　Spider 15
Eye
　Amphibians 30
　Beetle 6
　Bird 36
　Bony fish 6, 21
　Caiman 34
　Carnivores 42
　Chick 40-41
　Compound 6, 8, 10, 12, 13, 28
　Crab 28
　Crayfish 29
　Crocodilians 34
　Dogfish 18
　Dolphin 52
　Elephant 9, 49
　Forward-facing 6-7, 42
　Frog 6, 30
　Goliath beetle 8
　Gorilla 51
　Horse 46
　Iguana 9
　Insect 8
　Kangaroo 55
　Lamprey 18
　Lion 42
　Lizard 32
　Lory 8
　Mackerel 6
　Median 14
　Octopus 27
　Puff adder 8
　Rabbit 9, 44
　Rat 44
　Rattlesnake 33
　Salamander 30
　Scallop 26
　Scorpion 14
　Sea bream 8

Seal 52
Shrimp 28
Simple 14-15
Snail 27
Snake 8, 33
Spider 14
Squid 7
Terrapin 35
Tiger 6
Tree frog 6
Eyelid
　Caiman 34
　Snake 32
　Terrapin 35

F

Fairy shrimps 59
Falconiformes 59
Falcons 59
Falco tinnunculus 7, 37
Fang 14
Feather 36, 39
　Kestrel 7
Feather stars 22, 59
Femur
　Beetle 13
　Bird 37
　Butterfly 10
　Crocodile 34
　Domestic cat 43
　Elephant 49
　Frog 31
　Hare 45
　Horse 47
　Kangaroo 54
　Lizard 32
　Platypus 54
　Rhesus monkey 50
　Scorpion 14
　Seal 52
　Spider 15
　Turtle 35
Fetlock 47
Fibula
　Crocodile 34
　Domestic cat 43
　Elephant 49
　Hare 45
　Horse 47
　Kangaroo 54
　Lizard 32
　Platypus 54
　Rhesus monkey 50
　Seal 52
　Turtle 35
Fibulare 31
Filament 25
Fin
　Anal 6, 18, 21
　Caudal 6, 18-21
　Dorsal 6, 8, 18-19, 21, 53
　Lateral 7
　Pectoral 6, 8, 18, 20-21
　Pelvic 6, 8, 19-21
　Ventral 19
Finches 59
Finger 51
Fish
　Bony 6, 8, 20-21
　Breathing 20
　Cartilaginous 18
　Jawless 18-19
Flagella 24
Flagellum
　Beetle 13
　Snail 27
Flamingos 36, 59
　Beak 38
Flank
　Bird 36
　Cow 46
Flatworms 16, 58
Fleas 58
Flesh-eaters 6, 42
Flight feathers 36, 39
Flipper
　Dolphin 52
　Seal 52
Flukes 16-17, 58
Flying lemurs 59
Foot
　Bird 38
　Caiman 34-35
　Cow 46
　Duck 36
　Gorilla 51
　Horse 46
　Kangaroo 55

Slug 26
Snail 27
Tube 6-7, 22
Webbed 36
Forearm
　Gorilla 51
　Horse 47
Forefoot
　Caiman 34
　Tracks 56-57
Forehead
　Bird 36
　Dolphin 52
　Elephant 9, 48-49
　Horse 47
Foreleg
　Butterfly 10
　Caiman 34
　Elephant 49
　Lizard 32
　Terrapin 35
Forelimb
　Bird 36
　Frog 6, 30
　Hare 44
　Kangaroo 55
　Rabbit 44
　Rat 44
　Salamander 30
　Tiger 6
Forelock 47
Forewing 11
Forked tongue
　Puff adder 8
　Rattlesnake 33
Forward-facing eyes
　Carnivores 42
　Kestrel 7
　Tiger 6
Foxes 42
Freshwater turtles 54
Freshwater worms 58
Frigatebirds 59
Fringilla coelebs 41
Frogmouths 59
Frogs 6, 30-31, 59
　Eggs 31, 40
　Spawn 31, 40
　Tracks 57
Frontal bone
　Bony fish 21
　Chimpanzee 50
Frontoparietal bone 31
Fruit-eating bird 8
Fulmars 59
Funnel
　Lizard 33
　Octopus 26-27
Furcula 37

G

Galeocerdo cuvier 19
Gallbladder
　Domestic cat 43
　Rabbit 44
　Tortoise 35
Galliformes 59
Galloping 57
Ganglion
　Cerebral 9, 16, 27
　Crayfish 29
Gannets 59
Gape 52
Gaskin 46
Gastropoda 26, 58
Gastrovascular cavity 25
Gavialis gangeticus 34
Gaviiformes 59
Geese 59
Genera 58
Genital plate 23
Genital pore 17
Genus 58
Gerbils 44
Gharials 34, 59
Ghost anemone 24
Giant stick insect eggs 40
Gibbons 50
Gill cover
　Mackerel 6
　Sea bream 8
Gill filament 20
Gill opening 18
Gill raker 20
Gills
　Bivalves 26
　Bony fish 20-21
　Dogfish 18-19

Lamprey 18
Newts 30
Salamanders 30
Tadpoles 31
Gill slit
　Bony fish 20
　Dogfish 18-19
Giraffa camelopardalis 47
Giraffes 46-47
Gizzard
　Bird 37
　Earthworm 16
Gland
　Axial 23
　Cement 29
　Green 29
　Hypopharyngeal 13
　Mucous 27
　Musth 9
　Pedal 27
　Poison 14, 26
　Rectal 19
　Salivary 10, 13, 27
　Silk 14
　Venom 13
　Vitelline 17
Gnathostomata 18, 20, 59
Gnats 58
Goats 46
Golden lion tamarin 51
Goliath beetle 8, 12
Goliathus meleagris 8, 12
Gonad
　Jellyfish 25
　Octopus 26
　Sea anemone 25
　Sea urchin 23
　Starfish 22
Goniastrea aspera 25
Gonopore
　Barnacle 29
　Earthworm 16
　Sea urchin 23
　Snail 27
　Starfish 22
Gophers 44
Gorillas 50-51
Grasping tail 50
Grasping trunk 9
Grasshoppers 58
Greater blackbacked gull 41
Greater flamingo 38
Greater wing coverts 36
Grebes 59
Green gland 29
Green iguana 9
Green snakelock anemone 24
Grey squirrel 45
Grey whales 52
Grouse 59
Growth line 27
Gruiformes 59
Gulls 37, 59
　Egg 41
Gut
　Butterfly 10
　Honeybee 13
Gut caecum 14
Gynaecophoric groove 17

H

Haemal spine 20
Hagfish 18, 59
Hammerhead shark 19
Hand 51
Hares 44-45, 59
Harvestmen 59
Hatching
　Egg 40-41
Hawks 59
Heads 8-9
　Ant 13
　Banded milk snake 7
　Beetle 13
　Bumblebee 12
　Butterfly 10
　Caterpillar 11
　Frog 30
　Lamprey 18
　Pork tapeworm 16
　Rattlesnake 33
　Snail 27
Heart
　Bird 37

Bony fish 21
Branchial 26
Butterfly 10
Chimpanzee 50
Crayfish 29
Dogfish 19
Dolphin 53
Domestic cat 43
Elephant 48
Frog 30
Honeybee 13
Lizard 33
Octopus 26
Rabbit 44
Snail 27
Spider 14
Systemic 26
Tortoise 35
Heart urchins 59
Hedgehogs 59
Heel 46
Hemichordata 59
Hemiptera 58
Herbivores 42
Hercules beetle 12
Hermaphrodite duct 27
Herons 59
Heterocentrotus mammillatus 23
Heteropoda venatoria 15
Hind foot
　Caiman 35
　Tracks 57
Hindgut
　Crayfish 29
　Honeybee 13
Hind leg
　Amphibians 30
　Ant 13
　Beetle 13
　Bumblebee 12
　Butterfly 10
　Caiman 35
　Elephant 48
　Frog 30
　Hare 44
　Lizard 33
　Rabbit 44
　Terrapin 35
Hind limb
　Frog 6, 30
　Kangaroo 55
　Rabbit 45
　Rat 44
　Salamander 30
　Tiger 7
Hind wing 11
Hip
　Kangaroo 55
　Lion 43
Hippocampus kuda 20
Hippopotamuses 46, 59
Hirudinea 59
Hoatzin 59
Hock 43, 46
Holothuroidea 59
Hominids 50
Homoptera 58
Honeybees 12-13
Honeycomb coral 25
Honeyeaters 59
Honeyguides 59
Hood 25
Hoof
　Horse 46
　Sheep 56
　Tracks 56-57
Hoof bone 46
Hook 16
Hooked beak
　Blue-and-yellow macaw 38
　Common kestrel 7
　King vulture 38
Hoopoes 59
Hornbills 59
Horses 46-47, 59
　Tracks 57
Horseshoe crabs 59
House spider 15
Howler monkeys 50
Humans 50, 59
Humerus
　Elephant 49
　Bird 37, 39
　Crocodile 54
　Domestic cat 43
　Frog 31
　Hare 45
　Horse 47
　Kangaroo 54

(Humerus continued)
Lizard 32
Platypus 54
Rhesus monkey 50
Seal 52
Turtle 35
Hummingbirds 59
Huntsman spider 15
Hydras 58
*Hydrochoerus
hydrochaeris* 45
Hydroids 58
Hydrozoa 58
Hyenas 42, 59
Hyla arborea 6
Hymenoptera 12, 58
Hypopharyngeal gland
13
Hypural 20
Hyracoidea 59
Hyraxes 59
Hystrix africaeaustralis
45

I

Ibises 59
Icterus galbula 41
Iguana 9
Iguana iguana 9
Ileum
Bird 37
Frog 30
Rabbit 44
Ilium
Bird 37
Frog 31
Imago 11
Incisor teeth
Bear 42
Chimpanzee 50
Elephant 49
Lion 42
Rabbit 44
Rodents 44
Incomplete mesentery
25
Incurrent pore 24
Indian stick insect 40
Infraclass 58
Ink sac 26
Inner vane 39
Insecta 10, 12, 58
Insectivora 59
Insectivores 59
Insects 10, 12, 58
Body 6
Head 8
Intermediate pad 56
Internal skeleton 22
Interopercular bone
21
Intestinal caecum 17
Intestine
Bony fish 21
Butterfly 10
Chimpanzee 50
Cow 46
Crayfish 29
Dogfish 19
Dolphin 53
Earthworm 16
Elephant 48
Frog 30
Large 43, 50
Lizard 33
Sea urchin 23
Small 30, 33, 35, 43,
46, 48, 50
Spider 14
Tortoise 35
Invertebrates 58
Iris 27
Ischium
Bird 37
Crayfish 29
Frog 31
Isoptera 58

J

Jacamars 59
Jacanas 59
Jawless fish **18-19**, 20
Jaws
Dolphin 52
Shark 18
Snake 32
Jelly 40
Jellyfish **24-25**, 58
Jewel anemone 24

Jointed legs
Ant 12
Bee 12
Beetle 6, 12
Butterfly 10
Moth 10
Jugal bar 49
Jumping 57

K

Kangaroos 54-55, 59
Keel 37
Kestrels 57, 59
Beak 6
Talons 6-7
Wings 6-7
Kidney
Bird 37
Bony fish 21
Dogfish 19
Dolphin 53
Domestic cat 43
Elephant 48
Frog 30
Lizard 33
Octopus 26
Rabbit 44
Snail 27
Tortoise 35
Killer whale 53
Kingdom Animalia 58
Kingfishers 59
King vulture 38
Kites 59
Kittiwake 38
Kiwis 36, 59
Knee
Gorilla 51
Horse 47
Kangaroo 55
Lion 43
Rabbit 45
Koala 55, 59

L

Labial palp 13
Labrum 13
Lacertilia 32
Lacewings 58
Lacrimal bone 21
Lagomorph 9
Lagomorpha 44, 59
Lagopus lagopus 41
Lagostomus maximus 45
Lamprey 18, 59
Lampropeltis ruthveni 7,
32
*Lampropeltis
triangulum annulata*
32
Lampshells 59
Land turtles 34
Langurs 50
Lapwings 59
Large intestine
Chimpanzee 50
Domestic cat 43
Larks 59
Larus marinus 41
Larus ridibundus 41
Larva 11
Larynx 30
Lateral canal 22
Lateral dorsal aorta 19
Lateral fin 7
Lateral line 21
Lateral shield 35
Latrodectus mactans 15
Leaf insects 58
Eggs 40
Leeches **16-17**, 58
Legs
Amphibians 30
Ant 13
Beetle 6, 8-9, 13
Bumblebee 12
Butterfly 10
Caiman 34-35
Caterpillar 11
Crab 28
Crayfish 28-29
Crocodilian 34
Elephant 48
Frog 30
Gorilla 51
Kangaroo 55
Lizard 32-33
Moth 10
Salamander 30

Scorpion 14
Shrimp 28
Spider 14-15
Tadpole 31
Terrapin 35
Lemmings 44
Lemur catta 51
Lemurs 50-51, 59
Leontopithecus rosalia
51
Lepidoptera 10, 58
Lepidosauria 59
Lepidosaurians 59
Lesser wing coverts 36
Life-cycle
Butterfly 10-11
Moth 10-11
Limpets 26
Lion 42-43
Lionfish 20
Lip 18
"Lip" of trunk
Elephant 48-49
Little grebe 38
Liver
Bird 37
Bony fish 21
Chimpanzee 50
Dogfish 19
Dolphin 53
Domestic cat 43
Frog 30
Lizard 33
Rabbit 44
Tortoise 35
Liver flukes 16-17
Lizards 32-33, 59
Llamas 46
Lobsters 28, 58
Locusts 58
Loin 46
Loligo forbesci 7
Longhorn beetle 6
Lories 59
Lorikeets 59
Lorises 50
Lory 8
Loxodonta africana 0,
48
Lumbar vertebrae
Crocodile 34
Domestic cat 43
Hare 45
Horse 47
Kangaroo 54
Platypus 54
Rhesus monkey 50
Seal 52
Lung
Amphibians 30
Bird 37
Chimpanzee 50
Dolphin 53
Domestic cat 43
Elephant 48
Frog 30
Lizard 32-33
Rabbit 44
Snail 27
Snake 32
Spider 14
Tortoise 35

M

Macaques 50
Macaws 38, 59
Mackerel 6
Madreporite
Sea urchin 23
Starfish 22
Main pad 56
Major coverts 36, 39
Malacostraca 28, 58
Mallophaga 58
Malpighian tubule
Butterfly 10
Honeybee 13
Spider 14
Mammalia 59
Mammals 59
Carnivora 6, 42
Cetacea 52
Lagomorpha 44
Marsupalia 54
Monotremata 54
Pinnipedia 52
Primates 50
Proboscidea 48
Rodentia 44
Ungulates 46

Manatee 59
Mandarinfish 20
Mandible
Ant 13
Bear 42
Beetle 6, 8, 13
Bird 36-37
Bony fish 21
Chimpanzee 50
Crayfish 29
Crocodile 34
Elephant 49
Hare 45
Horse 47
Kangaroo 54
Lion 42
Rattlesnake 33
Rhesus monkey 50
Seal 52
Turtle 35
Mandrills 50-51
Madrillus sphinx 51
Mane
Horse 47
Lion 42
Maned wolf 43
Mantids 58
Mantle
Cavity 26, 29
Molluscs 26-27
Muscles 26
Scallop 26
Marginal shield 35
Marine turtles 34
Marine worms 16, 58
Marmosets 50
Marsupalia 54, 59
Marsupials **54-55**
Masseteric scale
Iguana 9
Lizard 32
Maxilla
Bear 42
Bony fish 21
Chimpanzee 50
Elephant 49
Frog 31
Lion 42
Maxilliped 29
Mayflies 58
Median eye 14
Median wing coverts
36
Mediterranean sea
anemone 24
Melon 53
Membrane
Chorioallantoic 40
Egg 41
Shell 40
Mermaid's purses 40
Merostomata 59
Merus
Crab 28
Crayfish 29
Mesenteric filament 25
Mesenteric perforation
25
Mesentery
Frog 30
Sea anemone 25
Mesoglea 25
Mesohyal 24
Mesothorax 13
Mesozoa 59
Mesozoans 59
Metacarpals
Bird 37
Bird's wing 39
Cow 46
Domestic cat 43
Elephant 49
Frog 31
Hare 45
Horse 46-47
Kangaroo 54
Lizard 32
Platypus 54
Rhesus monkey 50
Seal 52
Metamorphosis
Amphibians 30
Bee 10
Beetle 10
Butterfly 10-11
Fly 10
Frog 31
Moth 10-11
Metasoma 14
Metatarsals
Crocodile 34

Domestic cat 43
Elephant 49
Frog 31
Hare 45
Horse 47
Kangaroo 54
Lizard 32
Platypus 54
Rhesus monkey 50
Seal 52
Metatarsus
Scorpion 14
Spider 15
Metatheria 59
Metathorax 13
Metridium senile 24
Mexican mountain king
snake 32
Mexican true red-legged
tarantula 14
Mice 44, 59
Midgut
Barnacle 29
Butterfly 10
Honeybee 13
Milk snake 7, 32
Millipedes 58
Mineral spicules 24
Minor coverts 36, 39
Mistle thrush 38
Mites 59
Molars
Bear 42
Chimpanzee 50
Elephant 49
Moles 42
Mollusca 26, 58
Molluscs **26-27**, 58
Cephalopod 7
Mongooses 42
Monkeys 50-51, 59
Monodon monoceros 53
Monogenea 58
Monogenea 58
Monotremata 54, 59
Monotremes **54-55**
Moray eel 20
Mosquitoes 58
Moths **10-11**, 58
Motmots 59
Moulting 15
Mousebirds 59
Mouth
Barnacle 29
Bony fish 20-21
Cow 46
Crayfish 29
Dogfish 19
Dolphin 52
Earthworm 16
Elephant 9, 48
Frog 30
Gorilla 51
Horse 47
Iguana 9
Jellyfish 25
Kangaroo 52
Lamprey 18
Liver fluke 17
Lizard 32
Mackerel 6
Rabbit 9, 44
Rat 44
Sea anemone 24-25
Sea bream 8
Seal 52
Sea urchin 23
Snail 27
Spider 14
Starfish 22-23
Tiger 6
Mucous gland 27
Muscular septum 26
Mushroom coral 25
Mussels 26, 58
Musth gland 9
Muzzle 47

N

Nails 56
Nape 36
Narwhal 53
Nasal bone
Bear 42
Frog 31
Lion 42
Nasal cavity
Chimpanzee 50
Domestic cat 43
Elephant 48
Rabbit 44

Nasal passage 48
Nasal plug 53
Neck
Horse 47
Rat 44
Nematoda 58
Nephridium 16
Nephridiopore 16
Neptunides polychromus
12
Nerve cord
Butterfly 10
Crayfish 29
Earthworm 16
Honeybee 13
Ventral 10, 13, 16, 29
Nerve ganglion 13
Nerve ring 23
Nervous system 26
Nervous tissue 24
Neural spine 20
Neuroptera 58
Newts 30, 59
New World monkeys
50-51
Nighthawks 59
Nightjars 59
Nile crocodile 34
Nipple 54
Non-placental mammals
59
Nose
Horse 46
Lion 42
Rabbit 9, 44
Rat 44
Tiger 6
Nostril 8
Bird 36
Chick 41
Crocodilians 34
Dolphin 53
Domestic cat 43
Elephant 48
Frog 30
Gorilla 51
Horse 46
Iguana 9
Kangaroo 55
Lion 42
Lizard 32
Lory 8
Monkey 50
Puff adder 8
Rabbit 9
Rat 44
Rattlesnake 33
Seal 52
Nuchal plate 35
Nuchal shield 35
Nucleus 25
Nuctenea umbratica 15

O

Occipital bone 50
Occipital condyle 42
Oceanic seahorse 20
Ocellus 26
Octopus 26-27, 58
Odd-toed hoofed
mammals 59
Odd-toed ungulates 46-
47
Odonata 58
Odour 47
Oesophagus
Barnacle 29
Bird 37
Butterfly 10
Chimpanzee 50
Cow 46
Dogfish 19
Dolphin 53
Domestic cat 43
Earthworm 16
Elephant 48
Honeybee 13
Liver fluke 17
Lizard 33
Rabbit 44
Snail 27
Spider 14
Starfish 22
Tortoise 35
Oilbirds 59
Old World monkeys 50-
51
Olfactory bulb 21
Oligochaeta 58
Omasum 46
One-toed ungulates 46

Ootype 17
Opercula 20
Opercular bone 21
Operculum
Bony fish 20-21
Cnidocyte 25
Giant stick insect
eggs 40
Indian stick insect
eggs 40
Leaf insect eggs 40
Mackerel 6
Sea bream 8
Ophidia 59
Ophiothix fragilis 23
Opisthosoma
Scorpion 14
Spider 15
Opossums 54, 59
Virginia 55
Oral arm 25
Oral disc 24-25
Oral surface 23
Orangutans 50
Orbit
Bear 42
Bird 37
Bony fish 21
Chimpanzee 50
Elephant 49
Horse 47
Lion 42
Lizard 32
Platypus 54
Rattlesnake 33
Rhesus monkey 50
Orbital artery
Dogfish 19
Orb spider 15
Orcinus orca 53
Orders 58
*Ornithorhynchus
anatinus* 55
Orthoptera 58
Oryctolagus cuniculus 9
Osculum 24
Ospreys 59
Ossicles 22
Osteichthyes 20, 59
Ostium
Crayfish 29
Honeybee 13
Sea anemone 25
Spider 14
Sponge 24
Ostrich 36, 59
Egg 41
Otters 42
Outer margin 11
Outer vane 39
Ovary
Barnacle 29
Blood fluke 17
Bony fish 21
Butterfly 10
Chimpanzee 50
Crayfish 29
Dogfish 19
Earthworm 16
Liver fluke 17
Lizard 33
Spider 14
Tortoise 36
Oviduct
Barnacle 29
Butterfly 10
Crayfish 29
Dogfish 19
Lizard 33
Spider 14
Tortoise 35
Ovotestis 27
Owls 59
Oxygen 20
Oystercatchers 59
Oysters 26

P

Pads 56
Pagrus coerulostictus 8
Pancreas
Bird 37
Bony fish 21
Chimpanzee 50
Dogfish 19
Domestic cat 43
Frog 30
Rabbit 44
Tortoise 35
Pandas 42

Pangolins 59
Panthera tigris 6
Pan troglodytes 50
Paragaster 24
Parakeets 59
Parasites 16
Parasitic anemone 24
Parasitic flukes 58
Parietal bone
  Bony fish 21
  Chimpanzee 50
Parrots 59
Partridges 59
Passeriformes 59
Pastern 46-47
Patella
  Domestic cat 43
  Elephant 49
  Hare 45
  Horse 47
  Platypus 54
  Rhesus monkey 50
  Scorpion 14
  Spider 15
Pauropoda 58
Pauropods 58
Paw
  Lion 43
  Tiger 7
  Tracks 56
Pea fowl 59
Peccaries 46
Pectoral fin
  Bony fish 6, 8, 20-21
  Lamprey 18
  Mackerel 6
  Sea bream 8
Pectoral fin ray 21
Pectoral fin ray 21
Pedal disc 25
Pedal gland 27
Pedicel 13
Pedipalp
  Scorpion 14
  Spider 15
Peduncle 29
Pelecaniformes 59
Pelecypoda 26
Pelicans 59
Pelvic fin
  Bony fish 6, 8, 20-21
  Dogfish 19
  Mackerel 6
  Sea bream 8
Pelvic fin ray 21
Pelvis
  Bird 37
  Bony fish 21
  Domestic cat 43
  Elephant 49
  Hare 45
  Horse 47
  Kangaroo 54
  Lizard 32
  Platypus 54
  Rhesus monkey 50
  Seal 52
  Turtle 35
Pencil slate sea urchin 23
Penguins 36, 59
Penis
  Barnacle 29
  Dolphin 53
  Snail 27
Pentaradiate symmetry 22
Perch 20
Perching birds 59
Pereopod
  Crab 28
  Crayfish 28-29
  Shrimp 28
Perissodactyla 46-47, 59
Perissodactyls 46
Petrels 59
Phalanges
  Cow 46
  Crocodile 34
  Domestic cat 43
  Frog 31
  Hare 45
  Horse 46-47
  Kangaroo 54
  Lizard 32
  Platypus 54
  Rhesus monkey 50
  Seal 52
  Turtle 35
Phalanx 49
Pharynx
  Bony fish 20-21

Dogfish 19
Earthworm 16
Honeybee 13
Liver fluke 17
Sea anemone 25
Sea urchin 23
Phascolarctos cinereus 55
Phasmida 58
Pheasants 59
Phoenicopterus ruber 38
Pholidota 59
Phyla 58
Phylum 58
Physeter catodon 53
Piciformes 59
Pigeons 59
Pigs 46, 59
Pikas 59
Pinacocyte 24
Pinna
  Elephant 9, 49
  Gorilla 51
  Kangaroo 55
  Rabbit 9, 44
  Rat 44
  Tiger 6
Pinnipedia 52, 59
Placental mammals 59
Plains viscacha 45
Platyhelminthes 16, 58
Platypus 54-55, 59
Pleopod
  Crayfish 28
  Shrimp 28
Plovers 59
Plumage 36
Plumose anemone 24
Podicipediformes 59
Poison duct 14
Poison gland
  Octopus 26
  Spider 14
Polian vesicle 23
Poll 47
Polychaeta 58
Polymorphism 12
Polyplacophora 58
Porcupines 44-45, 59
Pore
  Cell 24
  Excurrent 24
  Incurrent 24
  Sponge 24
Porifera 24, 58
Porocyte 24
Porpoises 52, 59
Postabdominal spine 11
Posterior aorta 14
Posterior chamber of cloaca 33
Posterior dorsal fin
  Bony fish 6, 21
  Dogfish 19
  Lamprey 18
  Mackerel 6
Posterior sucker 16
Posterior tentacle 27
Posterior testis 17
Posterior vena cava 30
Posterior wing of shell 26
Potoos 59
Pouch 54
Pouched mammals 59
Prehensile tail 50
Prehensile trunk 9
Premaxilla
  Bony fish 21
  Chimpanzee 50
  Elephant 49
  Frog 31
Premolars
  Bear 42
  Chimpanzee 50
  Lion 42
Preopercular bone 21
Preoperculum 8
Primary flight feathers 36, 59
Primary remiges 36, 39
Primates 50-51, 59
Primitive mammals 54, 59
Proboscidea 48, 59
Proboscidean 9
Proboscis
  Butterfly 10
  Elephant 9, 49
Procellariiformes 59

Procyon lotor 43
Prolegs 11
Pro-otic bone 31
Propodus
  Crab 28
  Crayfish 29
Proscapular process 35
Prosimians 51, 59
Prosimii 50
Prosoma
  Scorpion 14
  Spider 15
Prostomium
  Earthworm 17
  Leech 16
Protein fibres 24
Protein matrix 24
Prothorax 13
Prototheria 59
Proventriculus
  Bird 37
  Crayfish 29
  Honeybee 13
Proximal pad 56
Pseudoheart 16
Psittaciformes 59
Psocoptera 58
Pteroclidiformes 59
Pterois volitans 20
Pterygoid bone 31
Pubis 37
Puff adder 8
Puffbirds 59
Pulmonary artery 30
Pupa 11
Pupil 34
Pycnogonida 59
Pygal shield 35
Pygidium 16
Pygostyle 37
Pyloric caecum
  Bony fish 21
  Starfish 22
Pyloric duct 22
Pyloric region of stomach 19
Pyloric stomach 22

Q

Quadrate bone 21
Quadratojugal bone 31
Quail's egg 40-41
Queen bumblebee 12
Quill 39

R

Rabbits 44-45, 59
  Head 9
Raccoons 42-43
Rachis 39
Radial canal
  Jellyfish 25
  Sea urchin 23
  Starfish 22
Radial cartilage 20
Radial nerve 23
Radio-ulna 31
Radius
  Bird 37
  Bird's wing 39
  Crocodile 34
  Domestic cat 43
  Elephant 49
  Hare 45
  Horse 47
  Kangaroo 54
  Lizard 32
  Platypus 54
  Rhesus monkey 50
  Seal 52
  Turtle 35
Radula 26-27
Raft spider 15
Ragworms 16
Rails 59
Raja clavata 19
Rats 44, 59
  Tracks 57
Rattle 33
Rattlesnake 33
Ray
  Branchiostegal 21
  Caudal fin 20
  Dorsal fin 21
  Pectoral fin 21
Rays 18, 59
Rectal caecum 22
Rectal gland 19

Rectum
  Bird 37
  Butterfly 10
  Chimpanzee 50
  Cow 46
  Dogfish 19
  Dolphin 53
  Elephant 48
  Honeybee 13
  Frog 30
  Lizard 33
  Rabbit 44
  Starfish 22
  Tortoise 35
Red deer 47
Red howler monkey 51
Remiges 36, 39
Reptiles 32-35, 59
  Body 7
  Head 8
Reptilia 32, 34, 59
Reticulum 46
Retractor muscle 25
Retrices 36
Rheas 36, 59
Rheiformes 59
Rhesus monkey 50
Rhinoceroses 46-47, 59
Rhopalium 25
Rhynchocephalia 59
Rib
  Bird 37
  Bony fish 21
  Crocodile 34
  Domestic cat 43
  Elephant 49
  Hare 45
  Horse 47
  Kangaroo 54
  Lizard 32
  Platypus 54
  Rhesus monkey 50
  Seal 52
  Snake 33
Rib cage 43
Right whales 52
Ring canal
  Sea urchin 23
  Starfish 22
Ring of trunk 9, 49
Ring-tailed lemur 51
Rissa tridactyla 38
Rodentia 44, 59
Rodents 44-45, 59
Rollers 59
Root of tail 46
Rorquals 52
Rostellum 16
Rostrum
  Beetle 9
  Crayfish 29
  Dolphin 52
Rotifera 59
Rotifers 59
Roundworms 58
Rumen 46
Ruminants 46

S

Sacral vertebra 31
Sacrum
  Crocodile 34
  Domestic cat 43
  Elephant 49
  Hare 45
  Horse 47
  Kangaroo 54
  Lizard 32
  Rhesus monkey 50
  Seal 52
Saddle 17
Sagartia elegans 24
Sagittal crest 42
Salamanders 30, 59
Salivary duct 13
Salivary gland
  Butterfly 10
  Honeybee 13
  Snail 27
Salmon 20
Sand dollars 59
Sandgrouse 59
Sandworms 16
Sarcophilus harrisii 55
Sarcorhamphus papa 38
Scale insects 58
Scales
  Bony fish 6, 20
  Caiman 34
  Cartilaginous fish 18

Crocodilians 34
Lizard 32
Mackerel 6
Rattlesnake 33
Snake 7
Scalloped hammerhead shark 19
Scallops 26, 58
Scaly skin 32
  Mackerel 6
  Snake 7, 32
Scape 13
Scapula
  Bird 37
  Bony fish 21
  Crocodile 34
  Domestic cat 43
  Elephant 49
  Hare 45
  Horse 47
  Kangaroo 54
  Lizard 32
  Platypus 54
  Rhesus monkey 50
  Seal 52
  Turtle 35
Sciurus carolinensis 45
Scolex 16
Scomber scombrus 6
Scorpiones 14
Scorpions 14, 59
Screamers 59
Scute 34
Scutellum 13
Scutum plate 29
Scyphozoa 24, 58
Sea anemones 24-25, 58
Sea bream 8
Sea cows 59
Sea cucumbers 22, 59
Sea daisies 22
Seahorse 20
Sea lilies 22, 59
Sea lions 52, 59
Seals 52-53, 59
Sea spiders 59
Sea squirts 59
Sea urchins 22-23, 59
Secondary flight feathers 36, 39
Secondary remiges 36, 39
Secretary birds 59
Seed-eating bird 8
Segment
  Butterfly 11
  Caterpillar 11
  Earthworm 17
  Leech 16
Segmented worms 16
Seminal receptacle
  Butterfly 10
  Liver fluke 17
  Spider 14
Seminal vesicle 16
Sensory antennae
  Ant 12-13
  Bee 12
  Beetle 6, 9, 12
  Butterfly 10
  Moth 10
Sensory forked tongue 8
Sensory structures 8
Sensory tentacle 26
Sensory vibrissa 9
Serpentes 32
Sesamoid bone 46
Shaft 39
Shags 59
Shannon bone 46
Sharks 18-19, 20, 59
Shearwaters 59
Sheep 46
  Tracks 56
Shell
  Chelonians 34
  Crab 28
  Dorsal margin 26
  Egg 40-41
  Molluscs 26-27
  Octopus 26
  Rib 26
  Rudiment 26
  Scallop 26
  Snail 27
  Terrapin 35
  Ventral margin 26
Shoulder
  Gorilla 51
  Horse 47
  Rabbit 44

Shrews 59
Shrikes 59
Shrimps 28, 58
Sieving beak 36
Silk gland 14
Silverfish 58
Simple eye 14-15
Siphon
  Octopus 26-27
  Sea urchin 23
Siphonaptera 58
Siphonoglyph 25
Sirenia 59
Skates 18, 59
Skeleton
  Ant 12
  Bee 12
  Beetle 6, 12
  Bird 37
  Bony fish 20-21
  Butterfly 10
  Cow's foot 46
  Crocodile 34
  Domestic cat 43
  Elephant 49
  Frog 31
  Hare 45
  Horse 47
  Horse's foot 46
  Kangaroo 54
  Lizard 32
  Moth 10
  Platypus 54
  Rhesus monkey 50
  Seal 52
  Snake 33
  Spider 15
  Sponge 24
  Turtle 35
Skin
  Amphibians 6, 30
  Frog 6
  Lizard 32
  Snake 32
Skuas 59
Skull
  Alligator 34
  Bear 42
  Bird 37
  Chimpanzee 50
  Crocodilians 34
  Domestic cat 43
  Elephant 49
  Gharial 34
  Hare 45
  Horse 47
  Kangaroo 54
  Lion 42
  Lizard 32
  Octopus 26
  Platypus 54
  Rattlesnake 33
  Rhesus monkey 50
  Seal 52
  Turtle 35
Skunks 42
Sloths 59
Slugs 26, 58
Small intestine
  Chimpanzee 50
  Cow 46
  Domestic cat 43
  Elephant 48
  Frog 30
  Lizard 33
  Tortoise 35
Snails 26-27, 58
Snake flies 58
Snakes 32-33, 59
  Bodies 6-7
Snipe 59
Snout
  Caiman 34
  Crocodilians 34
  Dogfish 18
  Rat 44
Snowflake moray eel 20
Sparrows 59
Spawn 30-31, 40
Species 58
Spermatheca
  Earthworm 16
  Snail 27
  Spider 14
Sperm duct 43
Spermoviduct 27
Sperm whales 52-53
Sphenethmoid bone 31
Sphenisciformes 59

Sphincter muscle 25
Sphyrna lewini 19
Spicules 24
Spiders 14-15, 59
Spinal cord
  Bird 37
  Bony fish 21
  Chimpanzee 50
  Dogfish 19
  Dolphin 53
  Domestic cat 43
  Elephant 48
  Lizard 33
  Rabbit 44
Spine
  Cnidocyte 25
  Dorsal fin 8
  Haemal 20
  Neural 20
  Postabdominal 11
Spines
  Sea urchin 22
  Starfish 22
Spinneret 14-15
Spiny anteaters 54, 59
Spiracle
  Caterpillar 11
  Spider 14
Spiral valve 19
Spleen
  Bony fish 21
  Chimpanzee 50
  Domestic cat 43
  Elephant 48
  Frog 30
Splint bone 46
Sponges 24-25, 58
Spongocoel 24
Spoonbills 59
Springtails 58
Spur 11
Spurious wing 39
Squamata 32, 59
Squamosal bone 31
Squid 26, 58
  Body 6-7
Squirrels 44-45, 59
Stalk 29
Stalked barnacle 29
Star coral 25
Starfish 22-23, 59
  Body 7
Starlings 59
Stelleroidea 59
Sterna hirundo 41
Sternal artery 29
Sternum
  Bird 37
  Domestic cat 43
  Elephant 49
  Hare 45
  Horse 47
  Kangaroo 54
  Seal 52
Stick insects 58
  Eggs 40
Stifle 46
Sting
  Honeybee 13
  Scorpion 14
Stinging cells 24
Stomach
  Barnacle 29
  Bird 37
  Bony fish 21
  Chimpanzee 50
  Cow 46
  Crayfish 29
  Dogfish 19
  Dolphin 53
  Domestic cat 43
  Elephant 48
  Frog 30
  Jellyfish 25
  Lizard 33
  Octopus 26
  Rabbit 44
  Ruminants 46
  Snail 27
  Starfish 22
  Tortoise 35
Stone canal
  Sea urchin 23
  Starfish 22
Storks 36, 59
Strigiformes 59
Strix aluco 38
Strongylocentrotus purpuratus 23
Struthio camelus 36
  Egg 41

Struthioniformes 59
Sturgeon 20
Stylet 25
Subclass 58
Subgenital pit 25
Subopercular bone 21
Subphylum 58
Sucker
　Blood fluke 17
　Lamprey 18
　Leech 16
　Liver fluke 17
　Octopus 26
　Pork tapeworm 16
　Squid 7
Sucking lice 58
Sucking stomach 14
Sunbirds 59
Superclass 58
Supraoccipital bone 21
Supraoesophageal
　ganglion 29
Supraorbital ridge 50
Suprascapula 31
Suture 50
Swallows 59
Swans 59
Swifts 59
Swim bladder
　Bony fish 20-21
　Cartilaginous fish 18
Swimmeret
　Crayfish 28
　Shrimp 28
Symphyla 58
Symphylans 58
Synchiropus splendidus
　20
Synsacrum 37

T

Tachybaptus ruficollis 38
Tadpoles 30-31, 40
Tail
　Amphibians 30
　Caiman 35
　Crocodilians 34
　Dolphin 53
　Hare 44
　Horse 46
　Kangaroo 54
　Lion 43
　Lizard 32-33
　Mackerel 6
　Monkey 50
　Prehensile 50
　Rabbit 44-45
　Rat 44
　Rattlesnake 33
　Salamander 30
　Scorpion 14
　Tadpole 31
　Tiger 7
　Tracks 57
Tail crest 35
Tail feathers 36
Tail fluke 53

Talons
　Bird of prey 36
　Kestrel 7
Tamarins 50
　Golden lion tamarin
　　51
Tapeworms 16, 58
Tapirs 46, 59
Tarantulas
　Mexican true-legged
　　tarantula 14
　Moult 15
Tardigrada 59
Tarsals
　Crocodile 34
　Domestic cat 43
　Elephant 49
　Frog 31
　Hare 45
　Horse 47
　Kangaroo 54
　Lizard 32
　Platypus 54
　Rhesus monkey 50
　Seal 52
Tarsiers 50, 59
Tarsomere 13
Tarsometatarsus 37
Tarsus
　Beetle 13
　Bird 36
　Butterfly 10
　Scorpion 14
　Spider 15
Tasmanian devil 55
Taste buds 8
Tawny owl 38
Teeth 8
　Caiman 34
　Canine 42, 50
　Carnassial 42
　Carnivores 42
　Cheek 42
　Chimpanzee 50
　Crocodilians 34
　Incisor 42, 44, 49, 50
　Lamprey 18
　Molar 42, 49, 50
　Premolar 42, 50
　Rabbit 44
　Rodents 44
　Tiger 6
Tegenaria gigantea 15
Telson
　Crayfish 28
　Shrimp 28
Temporal bone 50
Tendril 40
Tentacle
　Coelentrates 24
　Jellyfish 25
　Molluscs 26-27
　Scallop 26
　Sea anemone 24-25
　Snail 27
　Squid 7
Tergum plate 29
Termites 58

Terns 59
　Egg 41
Terrapins 34-35, 59
Test 22-23
Testis
　Barnacle 29
　Dolphin 53
　Earthworm 16
　Liver fluke 17
　Rabbit 44
Theria 59
Thigh
　Bird 36
　Gorilla 51
　Horse 46
　Kangaroo 55
　Lion 43
Thoracic vertebrae
　Crocodile 34
　Domestic cat 43
　Hare 45
　Horse 47
　Kangaroo 54
　Platypus 54
　Rhesus monkey 50
　Seal 52
Thoracolumbar
　vertebrae
　Elephant 49
　Lizard 32
Thorax
　Ant 12-13
　Beetle 8
　Bumblebee 12
　Butterfly 10
　Caterpillar 11
　Cirripedia 28
　Moth 10
　Wasp 12
Thornback ray 19
Thread 25
Three-toed ungulates 46
Throat 36
Throatlatch 47
Thrushes 36, 59
Thysanura 58
Tibia
　Beetle 13
　Butterfly 10
　Crocodile 34
　Domestic cat 43
　Elephant 49
　Hare 45
　Horse 47
　Kangaroo 54
　Lizard 32
　Platypus 54
　Rhesus monkey 50
　Scorpion 14
　Seal 52
　Spider 15
　Turtle 35
Tibiale 31
Tibiofibula 31
Tibiotarsus 37
Ticks 59
Tiger 6-7

Tiger shark 18-19
Tinamiformes 59
Tinamous 59
Tits 59
Toads 30, 59
　Tracks 57
Todies 59
Toe
　Bird 36
　Caiman 34-35
　Crow 56
　Duck 56
　Gorilla 51
　Lion 43
　Lizard 32
　Sheep 56
　Tracks 56
Toenails
　Elephants 48
　Gorilla 51
Tongue
　Caiman 34
　Chimpanzee 50
　Cow 46
　Dolphin 53
　Domestic cat 43
　Elephant 48
　Lamprey 18
　Lion 42
　Puff adder 8
　Rabbit 44
　Rattlesnake 33
　Reptile 8
　Turtle 35
Toothed whales 52
Tortoises 34, 59
Toucans 59
Trachea
　Bird 37
　Chimpanzee 50
　Dolphin 53
　Domestic cat 43
　Elephant 48
　Lizard 33
　Rabbit 44
　Spider 14
　Tortoise 35
Tracks 56-57
Tree frog 6
Trematoda 58
Trigger 25
Trochanter
　Beetle 13
　Scorpion 14
　Spider 15
Trogoniformes 59
Trogons 59
Trout 20
True bugs 58
True flies 58
Trunk 48-49
　Elephant 9
　Grasping 9
　Prehensile 9
Tuatara 59
Tube feet 22
　Sea urchin 23
　Starfish 7, 23
Tubercles

Sea urchins 22
　Starfish 22
Tubulidentata 59
Tufted duck 36
Turacos 59
Turbellaria 58
Turdus viscivorus 38
Turkeys 59
Turtles **34-35**, 59
Tusks 48-49
Twin-domed forehead 48
Two-toed ungulates 46
Tympanic bulla 42
Tympanum
　Frog 30
　Iguana 9
　Quail chick 41

U

Ulna
　Bird 37
　Bird's wing 39
　Crocodile 34
　Domestic cat 43
　Elephant 49
　Hare 45
　Horse 47
　Kangaroo 54
　Lizard 32
　Platypus 54
　Rhesus monkey 50
　Seal 52
　Turtle 35
Umbo 26
Under tail coverts 36
Ungulates **46-47**
Uniramia 58
Uniramians 58
Upcurved edge 39
Ureter
　Bird 37
　Bony fish 21
　Domestic cat 43
　Elephant 48
　Frog 30
　Lizard 33
　Rabbit 44
　Snail 27
Urethra
　Chimpanzee 50
　Domestic cat 43
　Rabbit 44
Urinary bladder 21
Urinogenital opening
　Bony fish 21
　Dolphin 53
Urochordata 59
Urodela 30, 59
Uropod
　Crayfish 28
　Shrimp 28
Urostyle 31
Ursus americanus 43
Uterus
　Chimpanzee 50
　Elephant 48
　Liver fluke 17

V

Vagina
　Chimpanzee 50
　Elephant 48
　Snail 27
　Spider 14
Valves
　Bivalves 26
　Scallop 26
Vane 39
Vas deferens
　Domestic cat 43
　Rabbit 44
Vein
　Beetle 13
　Butterfly 11
　Cephalic 26
Vena cava 30
Venom gland 13
Venomous snake 32
Venom sac 13
Ventral abdominal
　artery 29
Ventral aorta 19
Ventral blood vessel
　16
Ventral fin 19
Ventral groove 17
Ventral margin of shell
　26
Ventral nerve cord
　Butterfly 10
　Crayfish 29
　Earthworm 16
　Honeybee 13
Ventral scale
　Caiman 34
　Lizard 32
Ventral sucker
　Blood fluke 17
　Liver fluke 17
Ventriculus 13
Vertebra
　Bony fish 20
　Frog 31
　Rattlesnake 33
　Turtle 35
Vertebral shield
　35
Vertebrata 59
Vertebrates 59
Vertical pupil
　Caiman 34
Vibrissa
　Lion 42
　Rabbit 9, 44
　Rat 44
　Seal 52
　Tiger 6
Virginia opossum
　55
Visceral hump 27
Vitelline gland
　Blood fluke 17
　Liver fluke 17
Vultures 38, 59
Vulva 48

W

Walruses 52, 59
Warblers 59
Wasps 12, 58
Water bears 59
Water fleas 59
Water vascular system
　22
Weasels 42, 59
Weavers 59
Web
　Duck 56
　Frog 6, 30
　Kittiwake 38
Webbed feet
　Duck 36
　Frog 6
Weevils 58
Whalebone whales
　52
Whales **52-53**, 59
Whisker
　Heads 8
　Lion 42
　Rabbit 9, 44
　Rat 44
　Seal 52
　Tiger 6
White flies 58
White stork 36
White whales 52
Willow grouse 41
Wing
　Alula 39
　Bee 12
　Beetle 12-13
　Bird 36, 39
　Bones 39
　Butterfly 10
　Case 6, 12
　Coverts 36
　Developing 40
　Feathers 36, 39
　Kestrel 6-7
　Moth 10
　Spurious 39
Wishbone 37
Withers 47
Wolf 43
Wolffian duct 19
Wombats 59
Woodlice 58
Woodpeckers 59
Worker bumblebee 12
Worker honeybee 13
Worms **16-17**, 58
Wrens 59

XYZ

Yolk 40
Yolk sac 40
Zebras 46
Zygomatic arch
　Bear 42
　Chimpanzee 50
　Lion 42

Acknowledgments

Dorling Kindersley would like to thank:
David Manning's Animal Ark; Intellectual Animals; Howletts Zoo, Canterbury; John Dunlop; Alexander O'Donnell; Sue Evans at the Royal Veterinary College, London; Dr·Geoff Potts and Fred Frettsome at the Marine Biological Association of the United Kingdom, Plymouth; Jeremy Adams at the Booth Museum of Natural History, Brighton; Derek Telling at the Department of Anatomy, University of Bristol; the Natural History Museum, London; Andy Highfield at the Tortoise Trust; Brian Harris at the Aquarium, London Zoo; the Invertebrate Department, London Zoo; Dr Harold McClure at the Yerkes Regional Primate Research Center, Emory University, Atlanta, Georgia;

Nielson Lausen at the Harvard Medical School, New England Regional Primates Research Center, Southborough, Massachusetts; Dr Paul Hopwood at the Department of Veterinary Anatomy, University of Sydney; Dean Franklin; Roy Flooks

Additional photography:
Steve Gorton, Tim Ridley, Jane Burton, Matthew Ward, Jerry Young, Judith Harrington, Cyril Laubscher, Bob Langrish

Additional design assistance:
Simone End, Nicki Liddiard

Additional editorial assistance:
Christine Murdock, Louise Tucker

Illustrators:
John Woodcock, Simone End, David Hopkins, Sandra Pond, Nick Loates, Roy Flooks

Picture credits:
t=top b=bottom c=centre l=left r=right
Oxford Scientific Films/Animals Animals/Breck P. Kent: 16cl; 25tl /London Scientific Films: 16tr; 17tc. Sinclair Stammers/Science Photo Library: 17cb

Index:
Irene Lyford

Picture research:
Clive Webster